The TRANCE WORKBOOK

Understanding & Using the Power of Altered States

✧ ✧ ✧ ✧

KAY HOFFMAN

Sterling Publishing Co., Inc.
New York

Translated by Elfie Homann, Clive Williams,
and Dr. Christliebe El Mogharbel
Translation edited by Laurel Ornitz

Library of Congress Cataloging-in-Publication Data

1   3   5   7   9   10   8   6   4   2

Published by Sterling Publishing Company, Inc.
387 Park Avenue South, New York, N.Y. 10016
Originally published in Germany under the title
Das Arbeitsbuch zur Trance and © 1996 by Heinrich Hugendubel Verlag, München
English translation © 1998 by Sterling Publishing Co., Inc.
Distributed in Canada by Sterling Publishing
℅ Canadian Manda Group, One Atlantic Avenue, Suite 105
Toronto, Ontario, Canada M6K 3E7
Distributed in Great Britain and Europe by Cassell PLC
Wellington House, 125 Strand, London WC2R 0BB, England
Distributed in Australia by Capricorn Link (Australia) Pty Ltd.
P.O. Box 6651, Baulkham Hills, Business Centre, NSW 2153, Australia

Sterling ISBN 0-8069-1765-2

CONTENTS

PREFACE

I was initially drawn to trance by an allure to the exotic, which the West had lost for many people to a large extent. For me, trance offered an access to a "different reality" inseparably connected to the magic of foreign cultures. Writing about it reawakened in me memories of my travels through Morocco, Mexico, Brazil, Cuba, and West Africa, as well as time spent beneath the vast desert skies in Arizona, Utah, and New Mexico. I felt the need to tell people in the West about the many techniques I had studied, experienced, and practiced. I thought that the ecstatic experience of our own bodies would revive our respect for ancient cultures that had practiced an ecological way of life for centuries as a result of their interchange with their environment; I believed it would make us aware that although our civilization had made a great deal of progress, it had also made many sacrifices along the way. The main evil I saw in the persecution of pre-Christian cultures in Central Europe was the condemnation of their customs and traditions, along with the debasement of everything in them that went beyond a one-dimensional rationality and functionality. I wanted to fight this evil with a second Enlightenment of the "disenchanted world."

I rediscovered meditation, which I had initially learned to appreciate through Count Dürckheim. This time it wasn't so much Japanese Zen Buddhism that fascinated me—I was put off somewhat by the austerity of Zen—but the Tibetan Buddhist tradition. Of course, it was the sensory impressions that captivated me at first: The colorful ceremonies, masked dancers, expressive deities, and powerful music took complete possession of me. But as time went on, I developed a feeling for the more subtle contents, which I learned about through literature written with the Western reader in mind. I was impressed that this religion, which was really more of a philosophy, could survive in exile, and I was grateful that I was allowed to be part of it.

Certainly, one of the reasons I felt at home in Tibetan Buddhism was the major role played by philosophical reflection. It was here that I found the answers to the questions that had preoccupied me in a naive way as a child as well as later on when I was a philosophy student: Is there truly only one reality? And, if so, how can I be sure that my reality is the real one? However, my subsequent encounters with psychiatry and antipsychiatry in Italy, as well as my experience with psychoactive substances, had shown me so many realities that it began to seem to me intolerant and ignorant to speak of only one reality.

I had begun to respect every person in his or her own system of belief, no matter how strange, unconventional, or crazy it might be. Then I learned that reality is not an extraneous entity, but something organic inside us. We ourselves are the creator, participant, and observer of our personal reality. We create it, take part in it, and communicate it to others, and, at the same time, we have the ability to observe ourselves in action.

Our knowledge is governed by our interests, and these in turn are influenced by our character, as it is molded over the years. As Pascal, the 17th-century French mathematician and philosopher, said, habit has become second nature, and all too often it replaces our first nature, which we could get in touch with directly if only we allowed it. Frequently, however, we get entwined in the machinations of our own mind, which is constantly trying to arrange fleeting impressions into a significant whole in order to find meaning. This "manufactured" meaning offers support and structure and thus serves a purpose. But how much greater is the adventure of the mind when meaning is not manufactured, but is revealed of its own accord in an inspired moment? These moments give us insight into the true nature of the mind, which is open and unlimited. Once this insight has made us privy to previously unknown perspectives, it's difficult to go back to the prison of a self-manufactured meaning of life.

In my training in hypnotherapy, as developed by Milton Erickson, I found that the insights I had gained from Buddhism were easy to integrate. I began to laugh at myself, and I gradually got wise to my own tricks. I became aware of the "doer" within me knitting together and making up reality, pretending certain perceptions, evoking feelings, and getting absorbed in different philosophies of life. I got to know the inner participant who took part in everything the doer did, until the participant identified with the doer completely. The participant was so captivated by the game that it became a player against its better judgment. All too often, an inner voice would warn it not to take part, but the participant didn't want to be a spoilsport, and so it ended up playing the game again and again. Eventually, it was left to the observer to make note of the resulting catastrophes and to respond to them in its arrogant know-it-all manner. The observer had the annoying habit of always interrupting; it had to comment on everything. The observer was always one step ahead, and never truly enjoyed the present. Nevertheless, it could not

prevent the disaster of self-entanglement, although it had long since seen it coming. This reminded me of a Hindu myth about creation, in which the gods themselves create the world and then forget that they were the creators. They play hide-and-seek with themselves just for the sake of a little amusement.

One day I decided to join forces with my inner commentator, and asked it to let me know when I was about to become fixated on a preconceived view again or when I was busy collecting evidence to confirm my own prejudices. The trick was to ask the observer to let me know before suffering the consequences of my actions, not afterward. This made me more attentive. A wedge was driven between the periods of partial consciousness, or trance, and a path opened up ahead, giving me an opportunity to look behind the scenes. Increasingly, I was able to see myself moving from one negative trance into another in everyday life. Now it became necessary for me to gently lift and dissolve the spells.

Here, the Milton Erickson technique of hypnotherapy was very helpful. This therapy doesn't only deal with the human gift of using autosuggestion to get into direct contact with the unconscious and to use its healing, creative, and self-organizing powers. Nor does it only center on using relaxation techniques, which help us enter into so-called alpha conditions and achieve an optimistic feeling about being alive. It is just as important to be aware of our pessimistic and life-negating self-programming in order to finally emerge from these negative trances. Thus, this therapy includes a training in breaking the spells, or de-hypnotizing. It is not without reason that the sannyasin (Hindu ascetics) renamed hypnotherapy de-hypnotherapy.

To comprehend these ideas fully, however, it is necessary to have a transcendental understanding of the levels of being, including the Buddhist approach to self-liberation. If we have no other state than that of the trance, it is difficult to recognize it and more difficult still to free ourselves from it and awaken from the dozing state of our everyday habits. The transcendental perspective shows a free and conscious person that there is an alternative to being at the mercy of the contents of his or her own consciousness. New spaces open up outside our consciousness, spaces that lie beyond mere unconscious survival. However, only after we have acquired the taste for freedom can we look at the games of our unconscious and our consciousness in their endless variety, without taking them too seriously or wanting to endow them with eternal status.

Only with this playful attitude can a workbook on trance be written. In this context, "work" has more to do with approaching the subject competently than with any kind of toil or struggle. When I discuss everyday trance conditions, I mean all those states of mind, moods, emotions, tunnel visions, and daydreams—in short, conditions both conscious and unconscious—all those films that unwind and play within us. It will be important to observe how we fall under the spell of such conditions until we identify with them completely.

Once we become aware of how we entered a trance condition, we will also recognize the way out. We will learn to break the spells, to eliminate the negative "life programs" that prevent us from leading fulfilling lives. It is up to us to decide whether or not we want to do this; nobody can make this decision for us. A precondition of working with trance is that embarking on this journey must be totally voluntary. We hypnotize ourselves and are our own hero, who comes to our rescue, to liberate us.

During both light and deep, and pleasant and less pleasant, trances, you may come into contact with levels of your being previously unknown to you. They will only be revealed to you after all those layers have been removed that you thought were your real self but that actually only blocked your view of the larger dimensions. This, too, is part of working with trance.

I hope this book will provide you with refreshing insights and entertain you as well.

—*Kay Hoffman*

ABOUT THIS BOOK

I urge those readers approaching trance for the first time not to be too daunted by the large amount of information and the new terms, but to slowly read on. The Introduction will tell you about the many manifestations of the trance phenomenon and outline the historical development of the methods, and the Glossary toward the end of the book will explain the most important terms. Still, a lot of questions will certainly remain that can only be answered through actual trance experience.

However, you can simply immerse yourself in the pleasure of reading, thereby taking the first steps toward a better understanding. The exercises will be there when you are ready for them. Soon you will realize yourself that this is really a kind of dance. This book can be read from front to back or back to front or according to the topics that most peak your interest, without losing any of its "truth." It is important to understand that trance is never a question of belief; it is just a matter of experiencing it with your own body.

If you choose, you can do the exercises as you read along, because the theoretical discussions and the exercises supplement each other. There will never come a point at which your knowledge of trance will be complete, for the very reason that you will probably see everything in a different light as a result of the next trance experience. This is just the way it is, once you have let trance become an important part of your personal dawning of consciousness. Life doesn't stop being one huge dream and miracle. But it's best to have no fixed expectations when reading this book, but simply to wait and see.

INTRODUCTION

What Is Trance?

Trance is still conventionally defined as a state of reduced consciousness, or a somnolent state. However, the more recent anthropological definition, linking it to "altered states of consciousness" (Charles Tart), is becoming increasingly accepted. Over the past few decades, less of a value judgment has been made regarding whether these states are deeper or lighter or better or worse than ordinary consciousness. This means that usual, everyday consciousness no longer unequivocally ranks first, as it had for so long in the West.

Actually, the trance state should be discussed in the plural, because there is more than one altered state of consciousness significantly different from everyday consciousness. Some languages have different names for the various conditions. Naturally, cultures in which trance is regarded as a matter of course in social as well as religious contexts, playing a role in healing and inspiration, differentiate among trances more than we do. For us, the word "trance" still suggests something uncanny and strange.

Trances can be very light or very deep. They can have noticeable, even dramatic effects, or they can pass by unnoticed. Trances can happen spontaneously, or they can be consciously induced. Trances can in fact be kept under control and be employed in a controlled manner; however, they can also take on a life of their own and get out of control.

Trances are a common phenomenon among human beings. All of us have experienced trances in one form or another and know this state well. Do you remember when your mind was elsewhere—say, when you missed the highway exit or were so gripped by a play that time seemed to be standing still? It is possible for us in our waking consciousness not to have any memory of these trances. However, trance enables us to re-establish contact and uncover such buried memories. Trance also has the effect, more than anything else does, of exposing us to our ingrained habits and our lack of self-determination not caused by anyone else but ourselves.

When dealing with trances, it is important to respect your own nature, which has good reasons for developing certain automatic habits and reactions. But nothing is more restricting than showing contempt for your own ability to submit to the flow of life, to cultivate devotion, and to lower your guard for a while, all of which are elements of the trance state. In this context, you will experience trance as something healing, strengthening, inspiring, broadening, and calming.

If you devote your attention to trance for a period of time, you will eventually be confronted with the issue of your own spirituality, of getting in touch with your own source of being. Trance can only be used for "worldly" matters to a limited extent, even though it can be very helpful in such areas as management and coaching and self-organization. However, sooner or later, the question of a higher level of being will arise, and, because trance gives us a greater perspective, it will undoubtedly connect you to a higher level of integrity.

This means that trance cannot be employed selectively to serve a certain useful purpose. Trance strives of its own accord toward inclusiveness and unity. That is why working with trance is of such interest when dealing with a holistic understanding of the world and yourself.

The History of Trance

A well-known example of an old healing method employing trance is the healing sleep. This is an ancient religious ritual from Greece that promised healing and the solutions to problems, as did the oracles. A seeker of healing makes a pilgrimage to a holy place, where others had been healed before. One such place is the temple of Epidaurus, which you can still visit today. The seeker is received by a priest, who welcomes and blesses him. However, the priest does nothing directly to heal the seeker. He only has the function of a host. The pilgrim is made to feel secure so that he can concentrate fully on the healing process. Moreover, his expectations are raised, as everything is done to increase his feelings of hopefulness. The pilgrim knows that he will have a healing dream while sleeping in the temple, and he does. Contact with his inner wisdom is re-established in his dream, giving him the solution to his problem. Today, we use light trances instead of the healing sleep. These enable a patient to get in touch with him- or herself during sessions with a therapist.

Trances have been used at all times and in every culture, but especially in those that didn't have written records of their traditions. Fairy tales and myths were passed down from generation to generation, and they retained their vitality through their instantaneous renewal at the time the story was retold. Telling stories is in itself a powerful trance inducer, as most of us can remember from our childhood. But stories have to fulfill certain criteria if they are to enchant us. The have to reach us and affect us, and be written in such a way that we can identify with the characters.

It may well be that the stories of the saints that deeply moved people in the Middle Ages and took them outside the limits of their everyday consciousness are only of historical value today. But what legends do we have now that counterbalance the troubles and the limitations of daily living?

Our need for a renewal of our approach to a higher form of being that gives life meaning becomes even clearer when we take a look at the rituals we practice presently. Which of them still enchants and enraptures us? Which of them genuinely imparts significance to our lives?

In certain cultures, religious insights were solely passed on through rituals or ceremonies. Nowadays, such cultures are enjoying a renaissance of interest. Perhaps we are finally realizing how much we long for rituals and ceremonies to imbue our lives with meaning. However, as the anthropologists and ethnologists (for example, Felicitas Goodman) tell us, there are no traditional rituals or ceremonies that truly work and change our reality without the use of trance. Trance seems to be a necessary requirement for the transformative processes that rituals and ceremonies can produce. In fact, many of the rituals in present-day Christianity were once carried out in a changed state of consciousness. Not only the priests but the whole congregation went into a trance and truly experienced the holy event in their own bodies and minds.

Remarkably enough, a number of anthropologists and ethnologists today believe in the necessity of the trance experience, which they see as intrinsic to human nature. In the early seventies, the books of Carlos Castaneda triggered a flood of research and writing on—as well as a commercialization of—those societies in which shamanism is still practiced. Shamans traditionally use spells for the purpose of curing the sick, divining the hidden, and controlling events. Michael Harner, who was taught by the Amazon Indians, founded a school where many new shamans were trained. I had the opportunity to meet several modern shamans, like Eva Laurich, and I learned a great deal from them. Felicitas Goodman has also played a role in raising the image of so-called primitive cultures. Furthermore, she has shown that trance works across the borders of time, space, and culture.

But let's return to our own culture, which has been shaped by the Enlightenment. This 18th-century European philosophical movement brought on the era of rationalism, which influences our science and politics even today. Initially, this meant a rejection of the past, when people could use whatever power they had with next to no interference, but were not very much in control of their feelings. The Enlightenment was a major milestone in the struggle against persecution and suppression, and paved the way for the French Revolution. But even while rationalism was still celebrating its doubtful triumph in the form of despotism, surveillance, and renewed persecution and suppression, a countermovement was already emerging. The ensuing irrationalism expressed itself most convincingly in the romantic period. In many horror stories and Gothic novels, the characters moved inexorably toward their fatal end, like sleepwalkers in a state of trance. This interpretation of trance has had an important influence on the history of civilization, and it affects our idea of horror to this day.

The German physician F. A. Mesmer (1734–1815) developed a method that was named after him: mesmerism, which is also the origin of the verb "to mesmerize," meaning to enchant or hypnotize. Mesmerism is a kind of healing magnetism, with which Mesmer caused a sensation in pre-Revolutionary Paris. He announced the discovery of a subtle aura or fluid that penetrates and surrounds all bodies. According to Mesmer, the whole universe is bathed in this "agent of nature." He believed that illness was a result of obstacles that hindered the flow of the aura or fluid through the body, comparable to a magnet, and could be cured by a "smoothing out" of these obstacles. All that was needed, he said, was control of the poles, combined with a massage to support the natural effect of the aura. The healing effect of this mesmerism was often accompanied by convulsions, through which the imprisoned body tried to free itself. By means of this artificially produced crisis, the health of the person or his or her harmony with nature was re-established.

Considering the climate of the times, it is no wonder that mesmerism soon became a highly fashionable, albeit rather dubious, technique. In the spirit of liberation that prevailed after the Revolution in 1789, people enjoyed this "gift of nature" in what were known as Circles of Harmony, founded especially for the purpose. A new emphasis on the body asserted itself, connected, however, to a certain hysteria. Ladies fainted one after another during seances, because it turned out that the power of the aura actually had the effect of a serious overdose. Moreover, the relationship between the mesmerist and the patient allowed nothing short of a license for uncontrolled behavior outside of all social conventions. It is not surprising then that the dubiousness of the technique as well as the behavior associated with it fostered certain prejudices against the trance experience.

Helena Blavatsky (1831–1891), the founder of theosophy, was a historically important person who took a completely new approach to the phenomenon of trance. She was herself a trance medium with exceptional abilities, which she tried to put into practice in the Parisian cult scene. Here, however, she was repelled by the many charlatans who held sway in their city, and saw through their increasing exploitation. This prompted her to turn to non-European systems of belief, and especially to Indian philosophy, which she learned from teachers whose disembodied state meant that they could only be contacted during trances and in dreams. With this, she set an example and showed that not only could trance produce healing, but could also be a means of increasing the available information. While in trance, Blavatsky received messages from the hereafter, which she published in numerous writings. Theosophy was originally an association where exceptionally sensitive and gifted people met in order to place their abilities in the service of higher knowledge. Madame Blavatsky demonstrated through her own discipline and integrity that she was not governed by lower spirits or "astral specters," but rather that she had them in her power and moreover was able to make contact with beings on higher planes that possessed more knowledge and information.

However, the sensation-seeking attempts to exploit trance for reasons of personal gain continued. Around the turn of the century, everything abnormal exercised an immense fascination on the public. In addition to the first "freak shows," in which misshapen individuals were exhibited as fairground attractions, the phenomenon of hypnosis was now being presented on stage. People were hypnotized to flap around cackling like hens, and humans frozen in a state of suspended animation formed a living bridge between two chairs so that the hypnotist could walk over it. These are just two examples of how trance was being used to attract a gullible public. Thomas Mann writes about this in the novel *Mario and the Magician*. During such jamborees, there was and still is a great deal of talk about magic and supernatural powers.

The truth is, we are actually looking more at the exercise of power here, with nothing supernatural about it. Such misuse of potential healing has always been harmful to clinical hypnosis, because these theatrical displays inevitably placed the therapeutic use of trance and autosuggestion in a questionable light.

Finally, I would like to mention two people who had a formative influence on the image of trance: the Frenchman Allan Kardec and the American Edgar Cayce.

Kardec lived in the 19th century. To this day, the fresh flowers that always adorn his grave in a Parisian cemetery bear witness to his continuing popularity. People from all over the world make the pilgrimage to the City on the Seine to honor his memory in silent devotion. Spiritualism developed under Kardec's influence, especially in Brazil, and has been preserved as a popular healing method. Spiritualism affected such religions as Macumba, a polytheistic religion of African origin practiced primarily by Brazilian blacks, and a popular movement emerged offering an alternative to expensive doctors. But even people who can afford to pay for a doctor are turning more and more to spiritual healing. Apparently, spiritualism gives people hope and courage by means of devotion, humility, and a strengthening of their faith. Friendly spirits are invoked to fight the evil ones. A wise ancestor comes to the aid of the living, and here, too, information is received from the hereafter.

Edgar Cayce (1876–1944) has supplied the best example of a modern "sleep trance," which he induced through self-hypnosis. He would manage to fall into a sleeplike state before an audience and then, with a changed voice, deliver messages from the dead and from spirits. It is typical in such sleep trances for the medium not to be able to remember anything afterward.

Today, there are many trance mediums who "channel"—that is to say, they function as a channel for information from an out-of-the-ordinary reality. Some of them work in sleep trances that completely obscure the ego and after which no consciousness of the experience remains (total amnesia). These sleep trances have proven to be a great strain for the whole organism, so the conscious, or waking, trance is generally preferred. In this case, the mediums go into a lighter trance, which enables the ego to remain as a witness in the background and to observe what happens. The mediums remain conscious and in control of themselves. They can stop the trance whenever they like and cease to receive the flow of information. They are also aware of their own physical condition and of what is going on around them, and can react accordingly if it seems necessary. As far as I can judge, this condition seems to be one of extremely heightened concentration, which, though very strenuous, is experienced as pleasurable. In fact, sometimes such waking trances are physically quite refreshing.

When we are truly relaxed, the activity of the brain slows down from the rapid patterns of beta into the more gentle waves of alpha. In deep meditation, such as that employed in Zen Buddhism, an increased level of such alpha waves has also been measured. The boundaries between meditation and trance are fluid, and will be discussed in more detail later on.

Milton Erickson, the founder of hypnotherapy who died in 1980, introduced trance and hypnosis to orthodox medicine and psychotherapy—

hypnosis, here, is something different from traditional clinical hypnosis. Neurolinguistic Programming, or NLP, which is so popular today, is a further development of Erickson's hypnotherapy, for which, however, he failed to supply an orthodox methodology. Erickson would put his patients into a state of trance with the aid of little stories, and then would surprise them with the results of the distraction. While keeping the ego of his patients occupied, he would direct his healing messages straight at the unconscious, which he believed to have considerable self-healing powers. In this way, he healed himself of the paralysis that affected him when he was young and that he did succumb to in the end. He always trusted his unconscious more than his conscious self, and he applied this view also to the people who came to him seeking help.

These new developments in the use of trance, which differ from traditional hypnosis, have changed the way people see themselves. They are no longer simply victims of external forces, because they also create and shape their own reality. De-hypnotizing means to liberate ourselves with the help of trance. I notice that I myself am constantly in a half-conscious state. In fact, for most people, normal waking consciousness is nothing but a blind stupor. For seconds or minutes, I may experience a true wakefulness, but I know I cannot keep this up for very long. It is adequate, though, to give me a vision of the inner depths and possibilities that are there.

General Principles of Trance

Because the word "trance" tends to be associated with various expectations or anxieties, most of them exaggerated, it is well worth taking another look at some of the general aspects of the trance state.

Trance as a Process

Trance can be seen as a process with a beginning and an end if it is induced in a controlled way. This is not only true for all ritual trances in a social or a religious context but for therapeutic trances as well. The process of the trance experience is similar to entering and leaving a stream, in contrast to everyday reality, which appears static and rigid. During trance, the consciousness is a flow of information, a stream. A familiar term in the study of literature is "stream of consciousness," which James Joyce in particular tried to re-create in words.

This is an almost impossible undertaking, however, if we consider that the flow of consciousness happens at a speed of more than 200,000 nerve impulses per second. Every attempt to stop this flow in order to record it exactly is not only very strenuous but also goes against the natural capacity of conscious perception, which cannot take in so much so quickly. Therefore, it can be said that I am potentially in trance during every second of my existence, because I'm always connected to this great stream of life. Some people claim that they cannot go into a trance. But this only means that they are not able to entrust themselves consciously to the stream that has been carrying them unconsciously along the whole time.

Focusing in Trance

Trances differ not only in the levels of control that the ego retains or doesn't retain over the autonomic processes of the organism, but also in the levels of focusing and consciousness. We can produce a grid that is defined by the two coordinates conscious-unconscious and focused-unfocused. With the aid of this grid, we can place trance into four categories:

✧ conscious and focused,

✧ conscious and unfocused,

✧ unconscious and unfocused, or

✧ unconscious and focused.

The variant conscious-focused is equivalent to our waking consciousness, but only in its ideal form, because in waking consciousness we are rarely in a condition of concentrated focusing, which is necessary for top performance. Many people have poor powers of concentration; this ability has to be developed and practiced if you want to have it at your disposal when it is needed. It is not a natural talent or a permanent condition. On a physical level, it is equivalent to a state of increased muscle tension, which is not permanently desirable, but every now and then helps us to react properly—for instance, in situations where a our survival depends on a quick decision.

Most of the time, however, we are in a pleasantly cushioned state of dreaming and dozing, which is more like the conscious-unfocused variant. The conscious ego is fully awake, but the focus is not narrow but wide instead. This induces a feeling of relaxation and tranquility, which is experienced as a state of well-being. The dreamlike state can change, however, into a nightmare should the conscious ego lose control; then the soft, airy state becomes the only possible form of experience and the ego has no other choice but to watch helplessly as its consciousness, identity, and integrity dissolve more and more. This can happen under the influence of drugs or be triggered by illness, but can also result from tiredness, weakness, or other overpowering influences.

This condition is equivalent to the third variant, unconscious-unfocused, and relates to states of disorientation and depersonalization, which can occur, for example, after a shock or as a result of extreme emotional stress. Sometimes such states can become chronic and lead to ongoing mental disorientation.

The conscious-unfocused variant, however, is a light trance, which is usually classified under daydreams, dozing, and absent-minded reflection, and doesn't need to be taken too seriously. This is still a form of trance, but one that can, in a therapeutic context, be used in a controlled manner to induce inner search processes and bring unconscious knowledge to the surface in order to find possible solutions.

The last variant, unconscious-focused, is a trance with which most of us are familiar to varying degrees. It is the trance that keeps us under its spell and makes us obsessive, pushing us on in a state of compulsion without our being able to break the spell. In this realm we have little or no self-determinism. It's a state that includes every type of addiction or obsession, even those that initially may seem quite positive, such as that of the workaholic. This kind of trance—which manifests itself in the form of tunnel vision, dogged determination, extreme perseverance, unusual capacity to undertake stress, untiring endurance, or the mobilization of special powers—is dangerous, because it imperceptibly develops its own dynamics and soon governs the whole organism. It is well known that delusions and psychoses can give a person access to extraordinary energy and put one into a state of intensive experience. But the price for such intensity is high, and it is only a question of time until a breakdown ensues.

Thus, if we want to use trance in a controlled manner, for our own good and for the good of others, we have to be able pull off the trick of exploiting the positive sides of a particular trance while avoiding the dangers. To do this, we have to know what the advantages and the dangers are. The first step in the lifelong process of understanding ourselves is self-observation. As you embark on this journey, you will realize more and more, with a clearly focused awareness, how your consciousness has a tendency to fade out and how easily the focus becomes blurred. You not only will come to appreciate this increasingly, but you will also enjoy it and gradually lose any fears you may have had. You will have an experience that will touch you very deeply: You will feel like you are standing in the midst of life while being borne aloft at the same time; you will be able to rely on reality and cope with it even though, or perhaps because, you continue to flow. This may seem paradoxical, but once you start to entrust yourself to the stream of life energy, you will ask yourself what it was that kept you going up to now.

Monoideism and Monotony: The Principles of Traditional Hypnosis

Monoideism has to do with a devotion to one idea or thought; monotony is about sameness, as in a single tone. Both methods of induction work by sending the patient to sleep, thus switching off the differentiating waking consciousness. In monotony, everything becomes the same, because the stimuli hardly differ from one another, leading the patient's consciousness to the conclusion that everything is the same, so that the consciousness switches itself off. In monoideism, the focused consciousness is always offered the same thing. Here, too, the lack of stimuli causes the differentiating functions to be turned off. If we opt for an excess of stimuli instead of a lack of them, the reaction is the same. We are familiar with both a lack of stimuli and an excess of them from daily living. Likewise, we are accustomed to the results: common, everyday trances.

In the recent past, aesthetic and therapeutic demands for states of trance have emerged and produced new techniques. The glittering world of techno-discos, for example, offers highly aesthetic impulses, which are extremely stimulating for some people, even if they don't truly go into a trance as a result. The aesthetic appeal provides enough magic.

Although some ways of reaching the trance state are governed by monotony and monoideism, these are not the only approaches available to us. Another means of access is the conscious decision to go into a trance and the ability to steer your own consciousness into the desired state.

Neurological Trance Induction

It may well be that monotony and monoideism are a good means of working with states of trance to begin with, but at some point they become superfluous, because both the consciousness and the organism have grown used to putting themselves into a state of trance when they receive certain signals. What the stimulus means becomes more important than the stimulus itself on a neurological level. This is when we no longer have to switch *off* but can switch *over.*

✧ **Switching Off** This means suspending consciousness. Consciousness can be seen as a child or a slave of the unconscious and subordinate to it. At the first opportunity, it is afraid it will be taken over by the greater whole, the superordinate. When the consciousness is aware of its weakness and vulnerability, its fear of being overcome is all the greater. Being near the all-embracing unconscious is threatening and will be avoided whenever possible.

✧ **Switching Over** This refers to using your consciousness in its function of control and orientation. Now consciousness is seen as an equal partner of the unconscious. When the two work together, they can achieve incredible things— for example, when they gear guided daydreams to a desired goal and thereby strive to influence reality.

Between consciousness and the unconscious, there exists a certain division of work, which has proven to be very effective. The consciousness works slowly compared to all other processes that occur in the mind. The capacity of the mind is defined by the interactions of the neurons. Billions of possible interactions take place every second. However, thinking always lags behind. Therefore, in some situations, it is appropriate to set our behavior on "autopilot" so that it is controlled autonomously and thus takes place unconsciously. In other situations, such an autonomous control would be disastrous or at least a great restriction. Habits are difficult to change once they have been established. Every change depends on a conscious recognition of patterns and a deliberate breaking with these patterns.

Some trances depend on this state of autonomous control, in which everything happens by itself. This may have a certain fascination for us civilization-weary Westerners, believing that we are being transported back to a primal and natural state, which we thought we had lost. We are put in touch with something that forms part of our "basic equipment" as human beings, but that also developed in other species during the evolutionary process. In our brain, these functions of autonomous behavior control correspond to areas of the brain stem and the limbic system.

The cerebral cortex, on the other hand, is a new acquisition in evolution, whose consequences we cannot yet assess. Will we be able to use our intelligence in the form of self-awareness and apply it appropriately? "Cerebral trances" can, without a doubt, help us to admit and process more information, to develop better communication, and to harmonize actions and interactions according to the requirements of each situation. In this case, trance helps us to break away from our habitual ways, revealing visions of new territories. As a result of an activity of the brain that can be due to a trance state, even though you didn't actually go into a trance or experience a trance in the usual sense you can have a sudden insight or be flooded with new ideas.

Archetypal Trance Levels

Of the trances described here, you will find some more familiar and easier than others. It is important to know yourself well so that you can benefit from your personal preferences, inclinations, and abilities. Don't go against your own nature and force yourself to try something that you don't like only to prove to yourself that you are unable to enter a trance. "Go with the flow" here, and let your own nature show you the way. Don't try to act like an obsessive person if your nature is actually reflective. And don't force yourself into contemplation if you are basically a person of action and expression. You can experience the latter through trances of movement and creativity. Generally, we can distinguish three levels upon which trances take place:

✧ the level of inspiration (reflection, daydreams),

✧ the level of expression (ceremonies, rituals, artistic expression), or

✧ the level of activity (goal-oriented, but calm action, which is not solely motivated by the conscious will of the ego, from which it draws its strength, meaning that it is under the influence of forces that are often described as strange, extraneous, or obsessive).

In general terms, we find a historical development emerging here:

✧ from the archaic trance style of shamanism and a high expressiveness (which had the function of giving the audience access to "another reality" through convincing playacting),

✧ which led to the obsession cults, which in turn were an attempt to use the (magical)

influence of forces in a conscious and focused manner to achieve certain ends (here, the collective understands the lack of self-determinism prevailing during obsession as a contact with supernatural, demonic, or divine forces, which is the stuff of which myths are made),

✧ and which, finally, in an unobtrusive and quiet manner, culminates in an intuition that needs nothing but permission to turn inside—this, too, is trance.*

* From Jean Gebser's cultural philosophy, with its archaic, mystical, magical, mental, and integral divisions.

PRACTICE

The Benefits of Trance

When trance is used consciously, it occurs in a controlled and focused way. It serves a certain purpose and aim, and has its limits. It finds an appropriate framework, which defines its function, supplies a value and a meaning, and, at the same time, ensures that it doesn't break through its existing boundaries. In this way, we avoid a patient suddenly falling into a state of euphoria, madness, or illness.

Trance is not a "trip," as the word was used in hippie circles, but rather a journey with a return ticket. It is not a "magical mystery tour" or a voyage to the unknown. The process that will start to unwind through trance has a specific orientation: It is a means to gain access to particular areas of consciousness and inner spaces. Travelers have a "psycho-geographic" map at their disposal to help them find the way.

All cultures that work with trance have some sort of map of human consciousness, which may include the unconscious, the not-yet conscious, and the no-longer conscious. Shamanism, for example, has such a map. In hypnotherapy, there are also classifications of human consciousness. You travel into the past and the future by means of journeys through time. By traveling to the origin and the goal, you learn something about the greater frameworks that give a meaning to your life. In the course of the journeys to your sources and potential, you learn something about your possibilities, and by daydreaming consciously in search of hidden desires, you travel to the land of your innermost fantasies. This means that the focused and con-

THE PURPOSE OF TRANCE JOURNEYS

Through journeys into the body, you interrogate those parts of your personality that deal with life energy and health as well as point to disorders.

By visiting your emotions, you examine those parts of your personality that process information and thereby result in emotions.

Through mental flights of fancy, you achieve a better overview of things, and can then see into the distance better, to the limits of your own horizons; these limits in turn can be extended even further by such mental flights of fancy.

trolled trance is both a show of strength and a creative act.

We need strength to overcome our habitual lethargy, "to take off" and achieve enough acceleration to break through the limits of everyday consciousness. It is taxing to go into a focused and controlled trance, so you should never do it if you are feeling weak. What is being discussed here is the active trance. The passive trance is something quite different; it just happens, similar to running a temperature. The passive trance can actually have a refreshing and healing effect if you are feeling weak; in fact, it is often used for healing.

In a passive trance, the traveler is "picked up" and swept along, and it is up to the healer, shaman, or therapist to try to free the traveler from the spell of everyday trance and to carry him or her off into the broad expanses of his or her own possibilities.

The art here is to combine two principles that are essentially at odds with each other. Basically, trance is a process of liquefaction, a dissolving and breaking down of barriers. How can such a condition of openness be brought into line with established limits, ideas, goals, and frameworks? Although the emphasis here is on "work," we should really refer to it as "art" or "fun." It is the enjoyment of elegance and grace, of obvious ease and beauty, that immediately convinces and enchants us in the moment of their expression.

A special feature of the focused and controlled trance in contrast to other forms of trance is that it provides access to areas that are normally inaccessible to us. It is like a key to a locked door that leads into rooms of which we normally don't even dream.

ACCESS TO THE THREE LEVELS OF EXISTENCE

Trance supplies the following:

Access to the wisdom of the organism and to the autonomous autonomic processes of the body (self-organized wisdom of the body).

Access to the id level, where processes are predominant, everything is in flux, and both a continuum and chronic conditions can be considered. This level is marked by id events in contrast to ego identification: Whereas the id passes neutrally through the processes and keeps its energy, the ego takes shape through identification and thereby constantly runs the risk of considering processes as abstractions in order to give them names and treat them as objects (nominalism and objectification).

Access to the unconscious, by which is meant all knowledge to which you have no access at the moment. Thus, consciousness is a very limited and restricted area, where the focus of attention is on the object of which you are conscious at the moment, whereas the flood of possible knowledge is stored in the unconscious in order to avoid overstimulation. However, consciousness can be focused and controlled by trance, and thereby can gain access to that precise knowledge.

These three levels can be described in greater detail by being broken down as follows.

Unlocking Potential Through Trance

You gain physical well-being through:

✧ reducing tensions;

✧ finding the right way of dealing with pressure and stress;

✧ activating the immune system and self-healing powers;

✧ recovery and regeneration;

✧ achieving balance and harmony by centering and grounding;

✧ access to the senses and your own sensuality;

✧ sensitization, increased perception, and a healthy instinct;

✧ self-confidence and self-esteem;

✧ a positive relationship to your own body;

✧ inner and outer beauty;

✧ quickly overcoming tiredness and exhaustion;

✧ building up vigor;

✧ increasing stamina, coordination, and rhythm;

✧ increasing expressiveness and personal charisma; and

✧ having more self-assured manners, as well as more elegance and grace in posture and movement.

You gain emotional balance through:

✧ better contact with the unconscious;

✧ achieving distance from past emotions, referring to present emotions;

✧ dissolving fixed experience patterns;

✧ memories and recall of past experiences;

✧ access to forgotten positive experiences (happiness, satisfaction, success, fulfillment);

✧ dealing with key experiences that previously have unconsciously filtered perception;

✧ canceling out generalized knowledge by increasing the ability to experience;

✧ dissolving existential estrangement by experiencing vitality and presence;

✧ dissolving neurotic patterns of guilt and accusation;

✧ dissolving negative reasoning, fatalism, and self-fulfilling prophecies;

✧ appropriate response to grief, pain, and anxiety;

✧ appropriate response to situations of hopelessness, desperation, depression, and senselessness;

✧ bringing movement into situations in which you are stuck;

✧ having a positive attitude to life, as a process of constant change and renewal;

✧ having a positive attitude toward your own development and that of other people or situations;

✧ allowing transformation;

✧ reducing outside control, increasing responsibility for yourself;

✧ reducing extreme feelings of helplessness and/or omnipotence;

✧ reducing polarized either/or attitudes and black-and-white patterns;

✧ increasing tolerance, psychological strength, and sensitivity (differentiating nuances in the range of feelings);

✧ accepting complexities in the form of ambivalent feelings;

✧ examining your conscience more broadly by including all parts of the personality;

✧ questioning accepted systems of values and dogmas;

✧ clarifying hidden conflicts, realizing unconscious interests, paying attention to your own needs (especially for closeness and distance, or contact and self-sufficiency);

✧ developing self-respect and attentiveness;

✧ developing the ability to make and sustain contact or relationships, to give and receive love;

✧ increasing the range and the depth of experience, allowing the blending and the breaking down of barriers while keeping your own identity and integrity; and

✧ allowing intensity and ecstasy.

You develop mental competence, expanded intuition, and spiritual openness through:

✧ unconventional approaches that break through accustomed patterns;

✧ shift of emphasis, surprise effects;

✧ change of perspectives;

✧ introduction of the meta-level, which enables distance and provides an overview of the whole;

✧ access to all the knowledge stored in both the conscious mind and the unconscious;

✧ an integral approach, which allows the flow of learning and new holistic associations;

✧ conscious use of the potential of the right hemisphere of the brain, with its holistic, pictorial, and analogous understanding of facts;

✧ conscious connection to the left hemisphere, which orders perceptions and assigns them to concepts;

✧ training of synchronous results;

✧ stimulating conscious and goal-oriented search processes triggered by questions that go beyond the boundaries of logic and rational thought;

✧ experimenting with hypotheses that show the construction of reality as a self-fulfilling prophecy, and by which desired transformations are induced;

✧ learning new programs and unlearning old conditionings, related to success, luck, learning, and visions, as well as self-esteem and taking responsibility;

✧ competently handling possibilities to do with choice and decision processes;

✧ constant activation and actualization of the human potential;

✧ allowing synchronization and synergy;

✧ a new evolutionary orientation of humankind having to do with the integrity of universal truths;

✧ breaking through and dissolving established limits between humans and the cosmos, humans and the Creator, mind and matter, and energy and form;

✧ dissolving the existing view of the world; and

✧ having a broader understanding of ecology, which includes the inner and the outer worlds, translates all of evolution in the form of available information into globally linked interactions, and maintains stability within change, preserving a complexity of structure and a continuity of the open process.

Release from Negative Trances

Human beings are creatures of habit—but only in part. We are all familiar with the force of habit. But most of the time we don't realize how much we owe to these independent, well-worn, and ingrained sequences of action. Many things that we once had to learn the hard way have since become so familiar, so much part of ourselves and second nature, that we don't have to think about them anymore. This saves time and energy. Without the ability to form habits, the demands of daily living would be too much for us. Furthermore, habits give us the comfortable feeling of being at home in ourselves. In fact, the Latin word *habitare,* to dwell, is related to the word "habit." A habit is also a costume that is characteristic of a particular calling, rank, or function (such as a nun's habit) that protects the life within so that it doesn't have to express, identify, and declare itself. This saves time and energy too.

The power of habit only becomes an obstacle if it stands in the way of necessary change. Old habit patterns reflect old conditionings, through which we learned to adapt ourselves to our environment at that time in order to fulfill the demands then made on us. Sometimes it is necessary to carry out a rigorous checkup. We should ask ourselves at regular intervals which of our habits are still useful and which are really out of date.

Do our habits serve us, or do we serve them? Are we still acting independently, or have we become a victim of our own conditioning? The main reason why habits have so much power over us has to do with the fear of anything new, as expressed in the old saying, "Better the devil you know than the devil you don't." Often the hazardous business of searching for new solutions to old problems and conflicts seems too strenuous and not worth the effort, or the risks seem too high. And so we preserve the status quo—this is also a solution. In most cases, it is not the best one, but because it feels familiar we stick to it.

In order to avoid the constantly nagging feeling of uncertainty and indecisiveness, we convince ourselves that this solution is the only possible one. In this way, we protect ourselves from anything new and keep up this "self-programming" with great determination. However, in order not to expend too much energy on this, we enter into a continual state of trance so that our alertness toward considering anything new falls into obscurity. In this dreamlike state, we see sentences as if on a banner, like "That's how it is" . . . "There is nothing you can do" . . . "And besides, you can't change anything anyway." Thus, we remain the victims of a magic spell—a spell that we ourselves have cast.

Exercises: Breaking Negative Spells

Spells follow a certain logic, which reflects itself in particular language structures or patterns of speech. Many common phrases and expressions, by their very nature, have a psychological inference.

One powerful trance we are subject to is the "you trance": *you* say, *you* do, *you* don't, *you* know, *you* believe, *you* live—and thus you dwell entirely within the social trance of the "you identity."

Exercise
1. For a period of time, try replacing the word "you" with the word "I" and observe how the meaning of the sentence changes.

2. Take some time to think about how these changes would affect your everyday life if you were to draw consequences from them.

3. Write your observations down, and keep a record of them.

Another source of constant autosuggestion is repeating inwardly and semiconsciously: "That's just the way I am." The same identity is always being reprogrammed, and changes that could arise from new experiences can't influence or change these identification programs. The identity is cemented; it turns into its own myth.

Exercise
1. Complete the sentence that starts with: "I'm just . . ."

2. Take some time to explore whether or not there are exceptions. Note these down.

3. Consider how it would affect your image of yourself if you included these exceptions in your usual identity. Form sentences with these exceptions: "Sometimes I'm . . . (like this), and sometimes I'm . . . (like that)." Let them sink in. Now how does it feel?

4. Give those two identities names. Perhaps you'll find some other exceptions and even more identities. Give these names too. Write them all down.

Sometimes the power of habits can be so strong that the habits turn into myths. These myths may not only apply to an individual but also extend to a whole group: the family, clan, tribe, class, race, or nation. Myths have a way of creating preconceived ideas that affect our perception and prevent us from taking in things and people each time in a new and unbiased manner. We allow negative myths to influence us. Such an orientation steers our actions unconsciously and conditions our attitudes. It determines our expectations and perspectives as well as the radius of our horizon. It produces dogmas within our systems of belief.

Exercise

1. Can you find such myths and dogmas within yourself? Which sentences come to mind when you describe your original family (the family you grew up with)? Form sentences in which you describe where you come from.

2. Embellish your description with as vivid myths as possible, as if you were telling a fairy tale or singing an ancestral song.

3. Emphasize the melodramatic tone. Recite it in a loud voice and with exaggerated expression. How does it feel now?

4. Make a note of the tracks you've followed in this process. How far back can you trace the sentences? Who was it who always uttered such sentences? Describe this person, and be aware of your relationship to him or her.

5. What would happen if you were to say to that person that from now on you weren't going to cooperate anymore, that you were going to opt out of this system of belief, that you are the exception in the system? How do you think the person would react? And what would be the consequences for you? Note them down.

_____

_____

_____

_____

Mythical and mystifying statements express themselves in absolute terms and therefore often employ the following phrases:

✧ As long as I can remember . . .

✧ Always . . .

✧ In the whole world, wherever you look . . .

✧ Everywhere . . .

✧ Only . . . alone . . .

Exercise

Answer this question spontaneously without thinking for too long.

Do you easily become a victim of a certain pseudo logic, which keeps your thoughts under its spell?

Exercise

Fill in the following sentences:

✧ This is one thing that has never happened before, . . . _____

_____

✧ It never happens that . . . _____

_____

✧ Never . . . _____

_____

✧ Nobody . . . _____

✧ _____

. . . , anything else is out of the question for me.

✧ Either . . . or . . . _____

✧ _____

. . . —there is no solution in between.

Without hesitating, write down your associations in the order that they come into your mind. Let the completed sentences take effect on you. Feel the influence that this logic has upon you. When do the expressions somehow feel wrong? How do you notice that you have fallen for a pseudo logic? How do the absolutely exclusive words "never" and "nobody" affect you? How do you feel when you think or utter sentences using the "either/or" structure, instead of being more inclusive?

Exercise

✧ With a partner, take turns speaking "either/or" sentences. Make sure you are aware of the excluding positions you are taking, and stress the harsh, absolute separateness you are conveying. Then let these sentences take effect. Feel the nature of the attitude you are expressing. Is what you are saying correct? Does it feel right; does it feel whole and complete?

✧ Is there a gap, an objection, a hesitation, to be found? Express this without words through a posture, gesture, or movement. Emphasize the nonverbal expression. What is it trying to tell you? What does it tell your partner?

✧ Jot down your observations, impressions, and associations, and compare them with each other.

_____

_____

_____

_____

✧ Tell each other about your feelings. What feelings arise during this argument of pseudo logic? What other feelings could overcome or offer an alternative to these?

✧ From which everyday situations are you familiar with such logic?

✧ What new solutions can you think of for these everyday situations?

✧ What factors oppose such new solutions?

_____

_____

_____

_____

During another negative everyday trance, a chaotic condition arises and is maintained as a status quo. Confusion is a process that sometimes cannot be prevented, because it leads from one order to another, from the old order to the new. Literally, confusion means the flowing together of opposites. This means it can actually be a fruitful, creative process that leads to a new synthesis—but only if we go through the process and don't get caught in it. Confusion can be reproduced through the following language structures:

✧ Both . . . and . . .

✧ On the one hand . . . on the other hand . . .

✧ Neither . . . nor . . .

✧ And . . . and . . .

All of these deal with the coming together of opposites, which are usually separated and differentiated and thus mutually exclusive. It is as if two or more voices were talking at the same time, relaying opposite messages.

A feeling of ambiguity arises that can have a very destabilizing effect. In psychology, we speak of ambivalence if, for example, a person's physical expression is at odds with what he or she says. In this way, the receiver of such ambivalent messages, instructions, or even orders gets the impression that no matter how he or she responds, it can only be wrong. Most of the time, we react to ambivalence with frustration and resignation, which in turn produce the temptation to stay in this chaotic intermediate condition. All energy appears to be used up, every motivation seems to have disappeared, and the necessary change that could lead out of this distressing situation has become a distant wish.

Exercise: Conscious Confusion as a Healing Trance Technique

Find the time and space for a 10-minute trance. Sit down comfortably. Breathe deeply. Breathe into your stomach, and just concentrate on your breathing for a while. Feel how your breath flows into your hands, your palms, how your blood pulsates, how all your attention focuses on your hands, and how they become the protagonists of the trance game. Become aware of how different the two sides of your body and your right and left hand feel. Which hand feels stronger, healthier, more confident, better? Which hand is confused and indecisive, lazy, dark, passive, or even paralyzed? Sometimes the differences are clearly recognizable, and sometimes they aren't.

Then assign to the stronger hand the role of the "good hand." This hand contains all your potential for clarification, for finding solutions and making the right decisions. Now imagine a set of scales: The potential is on one side, and the problem is on the other. Instead of a problem, it can be a conflict, the feeling of being trapped or stuck, the quandary of not knowing where to turn, the frustration of not being able to get ahead, or feeling powerless to act. Place all your incapability and confusion in the other hand.

Decide strictly which is better and which is worse: the right hand or the left, and all that they symbolize. You know that both belong to you, to your situation, to life, just as both hands belong to the body. And now, after you have concentrated fully on the differences, close your eyes, and keeping them closed, move the palms of your hands toward each other until they meet. Take your time; this a valuable process, and it is important that you perceive it very consciously.

What we gain from this exercise is the truth that everything somehow belongs and fits together, even if our consciousness cannot quite grasp how. At first, this exercise is experienced as a process, a kind of approach. Then it changes its status and becomes a condition. Suddenly you feel, you know, that you have arrived at the condition of wholeness. The hands, for better or worse, are joined together. This is not a half-hearted compromise but a physical feeling of wholeness. You feel whole and together, even if you are still as confused as before. You have an inkling that the confusion represents a transition to a new, higher order. You are also aware of how content it makes you feel to have found at least the physical feeling of unity.

While still pressing your palms together and feeling the intimate unification of both sides, breathe deeply to lock the feeling of oneness deep inside your body.

Exercise: Body Trance—Feeling "in Order"

The objective of this trance induction is to conjure up and imagine the feeling of "being in order," or well integrated. It is a physical feeling. You feel it physically when you have arrived at this trance condition. You recognize it because you feel balanced, content, relaxed, and at peace with yourself. This has nothing to do with an order that may have been imposed on you from the outside and that is in accord with the ideas of others, perhaps of your parents, partner, or supervisor at work. This is your own order, which you can always re-create as a physical feeling, even if you feel full of contradictions, unbalanced, and not at peace, even if you are at odds with your surroundings and not in harmony with your fate. By calling up the feeling of deep down being in order on the level of your consciousness, you can enchant yourself with a spell of your own making.

The magic spell goes something like this: "However and wherever I am, and whomever I'm with and whenever I'm with that person, I'm okay the way I am." If you are religious, this self-enchantment may be easier for you, because you may believe that God accepts you the way you are. But even if you are skeptical and mistrusting, you can come close to incorporating this feeling if you simply recognize how beneficial it is for you and, moreover, what a positive effect it has on everyone in your environment. However pessimistic you may be, you can permit yourself this optimism for a certain time. If it truly does not fit into your belief system, you can merely look on it as a trance exercise or an important means of health care, something like brushing your teeth.

It's not necessary to repeat the spell verbatim as suggested above; the important thing is to sit down every now and then, breathe into your stomach, and tell yourself that you are okay the way you are, and then take a deep breath. In most cases, the relaxed deep breathing comes about of its own accord. At the end of the exercise, it's suggested to interpret the deep, free breathing as a sign to yourself that you are feeling totally okay and that your organism has always known this to be true, even if you or your ego are by no means ready to believe it yet.

Exercise: Eliminating Dogmas of Negative Everyday Trances

We influence ourselves negatively by saying certain things repeatedly. However, by altering these phrases or sentences, we also alter our basic orientations.

1. "I just can't help it."
(Autosuggestive programming for maintaining negative trances)
Positive sentence as a counter-spell:
"Today I *can* help it!"
Write down below your personal magic spell:

_____

_____

2. "In for a penny, in for a pound . . ."
(Programs that build up pseudo continuity by dictating consequences)
Positive sentence as a counter-spell:
"Today I don't want the pound."
Write down below your personal magic spell:

_____

_____

3. "Suddenly I am small, weak, and helpless again, like I was as a child!"
(Age regression)
Positive sentence as a counter-spell:
"Today I am grown up and I can do things differently."
Write down below your personal magic spell:

_____

_____

4. "And I thought it was only five minutes."
(Time distortion)
Positive sentence as a counter-spell:
"Time passes, and I follow along. I am here now."
Write down below your personal magic spell:

_____

_____

5. "Sometimes I am simply not quite there."
(Absences)
Positive sentence as a counter-spell:
"I am fully and completely there, whatever I am doing and wherever I'm doing it."
Write down below your personal magic spell:

_____

_____

6. "I don't know myself how I got into this."
(Daze, rut, and other fixed patterns of habit)
Positive sentence as a counter-spell:
"My ego needed a rest, and my unconscious is still new at this job."
Write down below your personal magic spell:

_____

_____

7. "It all seemed to unwind like a movie."
(Not being self-determined, being automatically programmed)
Positive sentences as a counter-spell:
"The world is a stage, life is a play, and I am co-writing the script. My unconscious keeps me entertained."
Write down below your personal magic spell:

_____

_____

8. "The devil just kind of got into me."
(Lack of self-determination through strong emotions)
Positive sentence as a counter-spell:
"Thanks to the devil, I have finally done something I always wanted to do without being directly responsible for it."
Write down below your personal magic spell:

_____

_____

9. "The first step is always the hardest."
(Inhibitions and blocks in processes and transitions)
Positive sentence as a counter-spell:
"Every beginning has its magic."
Write down below your personal magic spell:

_____

_____

10. "I simply cannot stop it."
(Absence of boundaries)
Positive sentence as a counter-spell:
"A creative break strengthens the dynamics of creativity."
Write down below your personal magic spell:

_____

_____

11. "Sometimes I ask myself what all of this has to do with me."
(Estrangement)
Positive sentence as a counter-spell:
"This is such a good movie that only I could have created it."
Write down below your personal magic spell:

_____

_____

12. "If I were a bird . . ."
(Illusory fantasies, evasive daydreams)
Positive sentence as a counter-spell:
"As a bird, I wouldn't be any different from a person on a flight of fancy."
Write down below your personal magic spell:

_____

_____

Solving Everyday Problems with Trance

The more you give up control in a controlled way and train yourself in the discipline of letting yourself go, and the more you train yourself to speak consciously to your unconscious, the easier it will be for you to keep a grip on everyday problems and to act according to the requirements of the situation.

I invite you to look upon going into trance as a way of doing what is best for yourself and for all concerned. It's important to hone your ability to enter the trance state so that you can use it in emergencies. But don't wait until an emergency arises. Practice while you are feeling so well and relaxed that you can calmly enter the unknown inside of you.

Solutions often present themselves as a result of simply letting go. However, letting go with your mind involves much more than, say, letting go of something you are holding in your hand. It is a condition affecting the entire personality, the organism, and the consciousness. In a state of light relaxation and calm wakefulness, the activity of the alpha waves is predominant, coming from the right hemisphere of the brain, which is responsible for intuition, creativity, and integral perception. In a deeper trance, which induces a deep relaxation, theta waves occur, which support imagination and visions. During sleeplike conditions, delta waves can be measured: These are said to be responsible for processes of regeneration and self-healing.

Therefore, trances in themselves are considered to be healing and refreshing. In addition, the use of trance is very helpful when it comes to dealing with many everyday problems. A few of them will be described here as examples.

Every example contains different proposals for trance induction. Make a note of which induction you would choose spontaneously, because this will tell you which one you would generally react to best.

Coping with Pain Through Trance

Like fear, pain is an important signal. You would be doing yourself a disservice if you tried to use trance to anesthetize pain. You are only truly coping with pain when you have accepted and understood the message of the pain and then made an appropriate decision. The organism has to feel that the consciousness is doing something to react suitably to the pain signal and to change the outer (or the inner) conditions. Only then is the ego ready to relinquish control and submit to the healing processes of the unconscious. Try to remember the last time you felt pain. Probably there was a first phase of uneasiness, when you wanted to find the cause of the pain. Once the cause was clear, it asked immediately for a reaction and this involved a decision.

Let's assume you decided to overcome your fear of the dentist and to make an appointment. What did the pain in your tooth feel like then? Certainly it didn't disappear completely, but it probably took on a different meaning. Whereas, to start with, it may have had the meaning of a diffuse threat, it now may have changed into a clear signal, into a demand for action. As soon as you responded to this demand, the meaning of the pain probably changed, and perhaps its quality as well. It is possible that, in addition to the voice of the pain, you then developed another voice that responded soothingly to the alarm of the first voice like this: "Everything has been done to understand the signal of the pain and to react accordingly, and everything will again be in order as soon as the dentist fills the cavity."

Most of the time, this second voice is stronger than the first, and even if the pain is still there, it is less in the foreground. When you understand the meaning of the pain, the pain retreats into the background, as if it wanted to say: "I have made my solo appearance, and now I am returning to the choir." And the choir sings soothingly: "All this is part of life."

This account doesn't involve a true trance induction. But the description of the process shows what happens to most of us when we feel pain. Of course, what we undergo is different in cases of chronic pain. However, with most types of pain, it can be said that the following general principles apply.

✧ Pain as an alarm signal is a stimulus, which calls for a reaction. The use of trance to deaden this stimulus is neither recommended nor effective, unless we are dealing with a chronic, unidentifiable pain or a pain to which there is no appropriate or healing reaction, like torture.

✧ Pain has a meaning. If the meaning is recognized, the quality of the pain changes. Here, you can even go one step further and proceed from meaning to reinterpretation. In other words, you can react positively to the pain and actually relish it (think of the gentle, agreeable pain during stretching exercises or massages, which helps the blood to circulate better through the clogged-up and hardened tissue). You can accept this pain as a sign that you are alive and that you have the ability to heal yourself (think of the tickling and itching pain of a healing wound).

✧ When overcoming pain, we are looking for the alarm signal that it contains. This is the job of the cognitive powers of our consciousness. Once you have recognized the pain and categorized it, you can start to reinterpret it. This reinterpretation is based on your voluntary willing-ness to enter into a trance state, which will shift the pain into the background.

✧ You can redirect your consciousness by elimi-nating certain sounds (or other impressions that affect your senses) that you usually associate with pain and fear and by replacing them with other, more agreeable sounds that suggest relax-ation and peace. By focusing your concentration on the agreeable sounds (or other impressions, such as touching, mental pictures, and memo-ries), you can blot out the disagreeable sounds. This happens with a method of trance induction used more and more frequently by dentists. By means of headphones, the noise of the drill is blotted out and replaced by the singing of birds, the splashing of a waterfall, or the sound of ocean waves crashing against the shore. However, not only does this call for competence on the part of the dentist but also the willingness of the patient to go into trance, which means that the patient has to have complete confi-dence in his or her dentist. But even then, the agreement of all your inner voices is necessary for this to work. This means that as a patient you will have had to do a certain amount of pre-trance therapeutic work in order to be attuned to yourself. And this is something that can't be expected of most patients.

✧ Distraction is redirection. Most methods of trance induction aimed at overcoming pain work on the distraction principle. However, everybody knows that a distraction like thinking, This is not as bad as I expected, is far less effec-tive than one in which we think, Hey! Look! There is a lion on the sidewalk. This means that the greater the stimulus our attention is redi-rected to, the more successful the distraction will be. If the distraction is only a common

pigeon strolling around outside, the pain will obviously retain the upper hand as the stronger stimulus. However, if the distraction is of special importance or interest to the person con-cerned—Isn't that a handsome man looking in through the window?—then the stimulus of the distraction will be stronger and can redirect the attention. This makes it necessary to find a stim-ulus that will have a strong effect on the person or one tailored to him or her that is stronger than the pain. But such a familiarity with the patient's personality and an understanding of his or her individual desires cannot be expected of the average dentist. Therefore, it is a better idea for the patient to be prepared to enter the realm of stimulating fantasies during treatment him- or herself.

Trance as a Creative Break

Give the unconscious a chance—sleep on things.

It has been proven that breaks can truly be creative even—or especially—when we are asleep. This knowledge is embedded in the organism itself, which is in dire need of breaks and takes one every now and then. Breaks occur when we are tired (even if we have slept enough) or exhausted (even if we have just come back from a holiday and think we should feel refreshed); they also come about when we are ill or feel bewildered, confused, indifferent, or detached, as if nothing could really touch us anymore. When we need a hiatus, we need "to let things rest and sleep on them."

What we are doing when we take a break, guided either minimally or not at all by our con-sciousness, is creating a space in which our con-sciousness can switch off and the unconscious can come into play. The unconscious runs at full speed, even if we don't notice it. The unconscious searches for solutions, compares possibilities, and points toward decisions; it activates self-healing powers and strives for wholeness, fulfillment, and presence, which we often cannot find consciously and try to invent by means of analytical thinking.

What's important here is the concept of switching *over* instead of switching *off.*

Whenever you want to switch off, pause for a minute and then imagine that it is a switching over that you want. When you need a respite, imagine flicking an actual switch or let an inner voice, signal, or message ring out in your head. Another alternative is to choose a certain piece of music that will play automatically in your imagination when you've had enough for the time being. Or perhaps there is even a particular memory—for example, of a pleasant holiday, a fulfilling journey, or impressions of nature—that you can think of when you want to switch off. Then once the signal has occurred, you simply switch over to the inner program of your creative break.

What is important now is to remember the physical feelings of happiness, the moments of deep relaxation. These sensory feelings store the information that belongs to the creative break program; they shape your present mood immediately as if you were reliving these feelings right now. In fact, this is actually what you are doing; by remembering, you are entering into your memories, and thereby attuning your unconscious to these agreeable feelings.

You put yourself into a trance, which places you in a state of relaxation and starts the process of unconscious problem solving and decision making. By taking a creative break, you delegate the tasks with which your consciousness cannot deal to your unconscious. A trance of this sort can be like a delegation to the unconscious. Of course, even here, you need to have a certain amount of trust in yourself and in the way your unconscious operates. No way can you take hold of, strengthen, and retain this trust better than by allowing yourself to let go, let the process unfold, while being awake and attentive at the same time. It is as if you were letting yourself look benevolently over the shoulder of your own ego, so that for a while the flow of life happens on its own without any outside help.

Reducing Stress with Trance

"Everything's just too much for me". . . "I don't know where I'm going anymore". . . "Stop the world; I want to get off!" Stress—we've all felt the effects at some point in time.

Stress is part of life. It is the body's way of responding to certain situations, and it makes considerable demands on the entire organism. Originally, stress had a survival function—that was back in the days when we still had to run away from wild animals, hunt down our prey in order to eat, and deal intelligently with catastrophes in the environment. The world was divided into hunters and prey. You either ate or got eaten yourself. Such were the basic stimuli that ruled our lives, and the organism dealt with them instinctively.

Are things that much different today, in our modern, civilized world? In some ways they are, and in other ways they aren't. The organism still reacts to demands from the outside world, even if they don't approach us in the same manner as before. But very often survival is still at stake, even if our understanding of what constitutes survival has changed in some ways. The process of civilization has imposed certain restrictions much to the benefit of the individual and of society at large, but these changes have not necessarily been good for our organism, which still believes it has to deal with wild animals and tidal waves. Generally we are not allowed to attack, and in many cases we are unable to run away. The organism is often not able to react directly and immediately due to a socially dictated suppression of aggressions and a blocking of the escape reflexes. Cognitive information processing comes into play and prevents spontaneity, by which we could react to stress in a natural way.

Within the nervous system, the sympathetic nerves ensure that the heart beats faster when we are in danger, in order to pump the blood to the extremities and to the muscles. This is because for us to be able to fight or run away, we need muscles enabling us to grip hard or run fast.

People who always live under stress never have the smallest respite; they don't allow themselves any kind of break, and such breaks no longer occur of their own accord. Here, the stress has become chronic and the regeneration phase is skipped. After a while, the effects of chronic stress become evident: exhaustion, lack of enthusiasm, weakness, deterioration on all levels, even sterility.

Conscious use of trance can help you order your unconscious to provide phases of rest and regeneration. The better you are able to communicate with your unconscious, the more pleasant and effective these phases will be. If the ego is alienated from the unconscious and from the organism with its auto-regulative wisdom, such phases of rest and renewal can be bypassed altogether, and without them you face the possibility of illness or some other form of crisis or disaster. However, you can prevent many illnesses or crises from occurring by entering into positive trances and thus giving yourself the respite you deserve.

Exercise

✧ Imagine that your organism has a built-in warning signal. This can be a red light that flashes before the fuses blow. Or it can be a whistle like that of a boiling tea kettle. Pay attention to these warning signals, to the flashing or the whistling, even before the signal has reached its full power.

✧ Picture a built-in indicator somewhere in your organism that gives you a precise reading on your "battery charge." Is your battery fully charged or flat? This indicator also shows when things are becoming too much for you and a break is overdue. In addition, it shows whether you are under stress or in a relaxation phase. Instead of a battery, you can picture this indicator as a wavy line on a chart. When the line goes up, an increase in demands is shown, and when it goes down, it signals a pause, rest, no overexertion.

If you feel that you urgently need a recovery phase, even a very short one, imagine the following:

✧ a wavy line that mediates between "up" and "down." You want to go from "up" to "down." In your imagination, you draw a line from "up" to "down" and allow your organism to follow this direction.

✧ If this picture alone is not adequate, add the physical feeling of moving downward. Remember the sensation of swinging, the phase of downward movement. Remember how it feels to dive, to become heavy and give in. The more consciously you can give in, the smaller is the risk of a collapse or a crash landing. Imagine a smooth landing with a parachute, even if this is totally out of your own experience. Your unconscious understands your mental picture. Try to find images of downward movement that suit you. Write them down here:

_____

_____

✧ Perhaps you will find it more convincing to imagine the stress situation as a deafening scream. Then this disturbing noise has to be consciously switched off. So imagine that there is not just an indicator in your organism that informs you of the stress-in this case, a scream-but also a switch that can turn the scream on and off.

✧ Imagine such a switch: Perhaps "off" is printed on the left and "on" on the right. "On" switches to activity. Maybe it is only a "power" button, which you switch on when you need strength. Possibly there is also a volume control, which can be turned down from the high-pitched screaming of an unhealthy maximum level to a deep, calming buzzing or bubbling. Instead of this, you could use certain mechanical sounds or people's voices. Or perhaps you know of some special music that can signal in your imagination that you now need to switch over and enter a phase of relaxation. Sometimes a single note is enough—for example, the sound of a gong or a bell. Jot down some ideas of your own for maximum and minimum sounds or signals.

_____

_____

✧ Perhaps you have certain memories of when the switching over was easy for you, because something occurred that made this possible, or it happened quite naturally and as a matter of course without your having to do much about it. Such a situation brings about a feeling of relief. Remember what it feels like to experience relief. What happens in your body? What kinds of sensations do you have? Write down your own corresponding situations:

_____

_____

✧ One example of relief is the feeling we get immediately after reaching a goal—say, you have just managed to catch a bus, and you lower yourself relieved into the seat. With relief comes the ability to breathe out (you might have been holding your breath) and to breathe deeply. There are probably other goals in your past that once they were reached, gave you a feeling of relief, although perhaps not as clearly defined. Which goals can you remember?

_____

_____

✧ What shows you that your organism has switched over to rest and regeneration? What features define this state?

_____

_____

Solving Sleep Disorders with Trance

What applies to reducing stress is the same for solving sleep disorders. The more you are in contact with your unconscious through trance, the more you will like the night, the darkness, and the condition in which the consciousness is switched off—meaning sleep.

As you learn to influence your brain waves at will through conscious trance induction—by learning to call up certain inner moods—the organism will start to react to small signals, like lying down, by switching off or switching over. Of course, there are other effective signals you can use, such as drawing the curtains, spreading a blanket out, and (with adults as well as children) a certain touch, like stroking the cheek, or a good-night kiss. The signals can be ones that reach the unconscious by way of hearing, like a mesmerizing voice telling a good-night story or inviting you to embark on a trance journey. Other indicators can be a calming piece of music or sounds with which you associate pleasant memories or soothing images, like that of ocean waves breaking along the shore or the murmur of the wind. Signs for deep relaxation can also be provided by inner pictures. You see yourself in a situation, whether from your own memories or in your imagination, that allows you to fall and stay asleep. Sleeping has to do with trust. Remember which impressions especially evoke trust for you. Jot them down.

_____

_____

A signal for falling and staying asleep can also be a certain physical feeling while lying in bed. Does the entire weight of the body feel supported? Is it totally given over to the ground? Of course, the weight of your body is not going to increase when you allow the feeling of contact with the ground, but the physical feeling changes notably. You no longer feel tense and pulled together, or contracted; what you experience instead is a sense of your blood warmly circulating throughout your body and a greater relaxation, which gives you a feeling of expansion. You may have observed that at the moment you fall asleep, your consciousness of your body—which previously had an outline and was held together as an organic whole by the fixed form of the body picture—now loses this outline. The boundaries seem to soften and start to dissolve. The weight of the body seems to drip to the bottom and loses its rigid form, exactly like a droplet. Perhaps right now, having read this analogy, you are experiencing a sleepy feeling spreading through your body. Try to recall this feeling when you want to fall asleep.

"To be in the arms of Morpheus" is a metaphorical description of sleeping, because Morpheus is the god of sleep and dreams. If you attach importance to words and images, and you can't fall asleep because too many thoughts are going through your mind, then don't count sheep jumping over fences but imagine that Morpheus is approaching you and beckoning you to the realm of sleep. Imagine the physical feeling of an embrace. Observe how your body reacts to this idea by opening up. Instead of giving, doing, and wanting, the body assumes a passive attitude of surrender, of being embraced and wanted. Imagine the god of sleep and dreams receiving and accepting you, and anticipate that every minute of your sleep will be a wonderful episode from a never-ending love story.

However, if you have difficulty indulging in such fantasies, then try thinking about duty. Recall the sound of the alarm clock ringing in the morning-a noise that immediately puts most of us in a state of apprehension and to which we often react with reluctance, tiredness, and the feeling of not having had enough sleep. How delightful are those extra minutes that we spend in bed after turning the alarm off. Put yourself in this condition of being allowed to drift but not for much longer, and, while under the pressure of having to get up, thinking: I'll just doze for a little while, have a little nap. The signal for the organism to get what it deserves before assuming its duty is "a little nap." Whether this nap lasts for five minutes or a whole night is not important; it is an organic phase in the "up" and "down" conditions between being awake and being asleep. Here, you can also imagine a wavy line, the curve of which dives into a valley and comes out symbolizing the nap that you allow yourself. You will be surprised at how much this idea of having a little nap can help you—that is, assuming you take the ringing of your alarm clock seriously, set it regularly to an early hour, and have to be at work at a given time.

Help with Search Processes Through Trance

Even if you are not suffering from the confusion often associated with old age or don't generally have a lack of focus or concentration, you are probably familiar with the following situation: You have mislaid something; you know that it is somewhere, but where? You search around bewildered, insisting that it must be here; it was here just a few minutes ago and suddenly has disappeared, although you are so tidy and always put everything away in the right place, but now it seems to be missing. . . . What follows are repeated searches through the pile of items on the table, emptying of the wastepaper basket, increasingly nervous rummaging in drawers and cupboards, walking around the room looking here

and there. . . . Logic doesn't seem to help at all, and there is nothing conscious thinking can seize upon to be rewarded with that "Aha" experience. There just seems to be a jinx on your finding it.

You think: The thing I'm looking for is hiding somewhere. I know it's there. I just don't know where. It's like a jigsaw puzzle: Everything is in front of your eyes, but you still can't find the missing piece. In cases like this, there is no point in trying further.

The only recourse now is to appeal to the unconscious. The unconscious not only knows that the lost or hidden object is to be found somewhere under the surface of what we can see, but it also supplies a way of tracing it. How often have you stopped searching and then, in a flash, found the thing that you were looking for "by chance" as if it fell right into your lap?

The imagination provides support for such search processes delegated to the unconscious based on the premise that "everything is there." And that's true—it's just the access that is missing. To enable the unconscious to create a picture of this as yet undiscovered existence, imagine a circle. This circle represents the left side of your brain, which perceives everything in a logical and organized manner, but doesn't recognize the existence of the object, because it "cannot see the wood for the trees," which means it is too focused on details. It's like the jigsaw puzzle, in which the piece is there, though hidden from you, because you haven't found the right way of looking for the obvious. Now imagine a second circle, which symbolizes the right side of your brain. This side has the ability to put together complex contexts and details in one picture that makes sense.

By employing this trance technique, you can visualize the abilities of both halves of your brain and use them. First you recognize that something is missing. Next you acknowledge that the missing object exists but you have no access to it. At this point, you have to be patient and wait trustingly until the unconscious or your intuition searches for the missing object and then traces the way to it. Now all you have to do to find it is to follow the track with your consciousness or let yourself be led by your unconscious. This process may seem a bit mysterious, but it works.

If you don't especially relate to this mind-picture trance technique, there is another method you can use that employs deep, calm breathing. Faced with a lost or missing object, instead of panicking you just sit down and breathe calmly, telling yourself or perhaps singing to yourself: Everything is there. The question is, where? This will enable you to achieve a calm, composed state of mind, which makes the search process easier. You move the search process from the outside to the inside, from the left half of the brain—which is responsible for exact, detailed searching according to the chronological principle of "one thing after the other"—to the right side of the brain—responsible for clever tricks, unpredictable ideas and fantasies, and solutions that may be completely illogical but still right on target. By confronting the negative panic trance you are in with a naive ease and then entering a carefree, childlike trance, you will be able to help your unconscious fully exploit its abilities.

You may not believe it, but singing really helps! Of course, you can also talk to yourself, as long as what you say is something nice and soothing.

Once I read about a trance induction in which you only had to say to yourself: Tut, tut, tut, where is it then, where is it then? Tut, tut, tut, what am I going to do? Ttttttt, what's the meaning of this? Along with this, you can shake your head slightly. This way, you get a perfect picture of a confused person who is nevertheless at one with him- or herself. Countless successful detectives behave in this likeable, dopey way before they surprise us with their precise solutions!

Another method that has proven to be highly effective is humor. The ability to laugh at yourself makes search processes much easier, and it also provides an interesting challenge in daily living, in which routine normally serves up everything in a "prepackaged," or expected, manner.

Trance as an Aid in Decision Making

This trance technique carries on where the last one left off, and involves the visualization of a circle and deep, calm breathing. Its aim is to dissolve conditions in which we feel confused, distracted, and indecisive, and are unable to make decisions.

In this case, breathing into the stomach is important: The deep, relaxed breathing into the stomach takes us involuntarily back to our childhood (usually before we started school) to a condition of openness and naivete, in which everything seemed miraculous and nothing seemed impossible.

Exercise

Take some time to sit down comfortably and close your eyes.

Put your hands on your stomach, and feel your deep breaths moving in waves; now lift the abdominal wall just slightly, and then pull it back down again. Listen to the sound of your breath. Your eyes can be closed or half open, with heavy, relaxed eyelids, looking down diagonally. Your mouth can be open slightly, so that the jaws hang down a bit and your mouth waters because you are so pleasantly relaxed.

Your stomach feels like a smooth, round ball, and your pelvis, with its large, protective bones, is like a bowl, into which you can let all the tension flow that has collected inside of you, everything that has jammed up and been locked in, or restricted. Let it all flow down with the breath and gravity into the bottom of your pelvis and collect there. Let everything flow to the lower part of your body, where you are in contact with the chair you are sitting on. Imagine this area as the collecting bowl of your unconscious, where everything settles like ground water.

Now imagine drawing a circle around yourself. Your entire negative condition—all your indecisive, half-hearted attempts to act, all your different vacillations this way and that—are inside this circle. In your imagination, they might take on the appearance of scraps of paper, a gray veil, or tattered fringes. You might have a particular physical sensation that relates to this condition. Or you could hear it as a babble of voices. What emerges is a clearly delineated picture, even if everything inside it looks, feels, or sounds confused and chaotic.

It is one great whole. And you know that in some way everything belongs together. It is all part of yourself, whether you like it or not. However, by collecting and putting it all inside a large circle, you have already regained some control, even if it is only in your imagination. Now produce more circles within this circle as well as a center point, like on an archer's target. When you hit this center, you have "scored a bull's-eye." Imagine this feeling of hitting the center, of scoring a bull's-eye. You may not be able to feel this at first, perhaps because you have never shot an arrow. But your unconscious knows enough about it to distinguish what is closer to the middle, the bull's-eye, and what is further away. The mere picture of a circle with a center is enough to give the unconscious the order to create a differentiated idea of what is important and what isn't. You also have the opportunity to make "gut decisions"—in other words, to base your decisions on intuition or emotion instead of on logic and reason. Of course, intellect and intuition are an ideal combination for making good and well-founded decisions.

However, the beginning of the decision-making process should be left up to the unconscious. This is especially true when the pressure of being indecisive and the inability to make a decision have increased and you can't see any way backward or forward. When it feels as if there's no solution in sight—not even in your wildest imagination—then the time has come to move to a different level by concentrating on the target. Just contemplating this symbol creates a certain meaning—even if we are not aware of it consciously. Contemplation is an inner search process that is adopted by the unconscious, and its first effect is concentration, albeit on the level of form rather than content. However, the form discovers its content—even if we are used to the process happening the other way around. This technique has been shown to work time after time, regardless of how strange it may seem at first.

Solving Relationship Problems with Trance

When problems arise in a relationship, they often appear in the form of negative trances. The technique that follows is designed to help you deal with situations of seemingly unsolvable entanglement, or clinch situations, the word "clinch" being derived from the boxing expression for a stalemate hold that prevents any further movement. It is a technique that requires a certain amount of ability to concentrate and visualize, and you do it alone. It affects the structure of the relationship in an almost magical way, dissolving the clinch without the use of force or manipulation.

Exercise

Devote about five minutes of time to this exercise every day, perhaps for a week, or even longer if you have a lot of staying power. Always choose the same time of day for the exercise. Make sure you are relaxed and sitting comfortably, and take care that nothing disturbs you. Don't break off in the middle of the exercise, but follow it through to the end. Approach what occurs as an experiment, leaving the conclusion (the question of what is going to happen with the relationship) open-ended. Concentrate fully on the inner events that the exercise triggers in your emotional life, including those that have to do with a relationship you want to improve or with your connection to the outside world in general. Try to stay in a relaxed, casual, and tension-free state of mind throughout the exercise, regardless of what happens and what insights you may acquire.

Begin the exercise by imagining a circle. Now picture the circle being filled with golden light: It starts to shine with ever greater radiance. Perhaps this image alone will put you in a blissful state of inner richness. Next imagine yourself sitting down in this circle, inside this golden light, and bathing in it. Consciously let the golden light influence your state of mind. You allow yourself to merge with the light, thereby radiating a golden aura yourself. You experience the richness, the abundance, of the light, and it makes you feel almost euphoric. Once you have taken in and absorbed the golden vibrations as if they were food, and you feel thoroughly penetrated by them, then imagine a blue ring around the golden circle, a ring that is pleasantly cool, light, and flowing. Make sure that the blue ring is neither muted and murky nor rigid and frozen but remains clear and flowing. Now imagine carefully tracing the blue outline of the circle clockwise with your finger, and feel how this changes your physical sensation. The golden light keeps on glowing, but it is now combined with the cooling element of the blue outline.

When this inner picture feels satisfying and has achieved a harmonious balance of the polarized forces inside of you, then visualize another circle outside of your own. This circle is also filled with golden light and starts to shine. When the radiance has increased to the point at which it overflows the limits of the circle, then imagine the person with whom you want to improve your relationship entering this circle and sitting down in the middle.

This person is also filled by the surrounding golden light and encompassed within an outer circle of flowing blue. He or she may react differently from the way you anticipated. The circle may move—overlapping your own circle or sliding out of your line of vision. Keep bringing the circle back so that it is close to your own circle, and make sure that the blue color as well as the gold keep on shining. The gold represents the value we see in ourselves, and the blue our limitations. In both cases, the gold should completely fill the circle and radiate a warming glow, whereas the blue with its clear shine encompasses the gold like the setting of a jewel in a ring. Only when you can visualize both circles shining, but separate from each other, and only when the two circles have achieved a balance in relationship to each other that is acceptable to you, can you proceed to let the other circle join yours, but just in such a way that both circles merely touch momentarily along the outer blue shell. You may experience this contact as soon as it happens like an electric charge or flying sparks. In this case, the contact is alive and coherent. Both circles should charge each other but at the same time maintain their distance, and this calls for a balance that needs a lot of attention. Even in your imagination, you will feel how much sensitivity and flexibility as well as inner calmness and concentration this balance requires in order to re-create itself continuously.

Do this imagination exercise carefully, step by step, every day. Here, too, you will be surprised at what the power of visualization can achieve!

By the way, this exercise can be beneficial even if you aren't in a problematic relationship. It can have a positive effect on your state of mind as well as on your attitude toward the outside world.

Types of Creative Trance

The word "creativity" fills many people with a feeling of deep respect. Creativity seems to be a gift with which only a few chosen people are endowed. Many people regard creativity as something that others have and that they cannot make use of themselves. The creativity of others has, in fact, become consumer items. Scarcely anyone, outside of an artist, writer, or composer, for example, would think of being creative him- or herself. Yet daily living supplies numerous opportunities for us to be creative in order to cope with our lives. Time and again we are faced with problematic situations or people, and there are few precedents we can use to help us get our bearings, few laws or regulations with which we simply have to comply in order to act correctly. If we ask for advice, we may receive it, although if we act blindly on such advice, without taking the trouble to think for ourselves, we more often than not will find ourselves off track. In these tricky situations, we are usually on our own and have to find solutions that feel right for us.

Generally, it is more of a feeling or a perception than reasoning that is required in these cases. At the same time, it is not a matter of discovering something completely new. The solutions are often there already; we just have to find them. But our view is blocked so that we "can't see the forest for the trees." As often as not, we end up racking our brains because we can't think, almost pulling out our hair in desperation.

In this section, I'm going to introduce you to a completely different way of solving problems. We will start from the premise that problems will solve themselves if we allow them to. This may seem simple, but it isn't. Letting go, letting things happen, is especially difficult for us, because we are usually not calm or relaxed enough. But we can consciously recapture this calmness, which we seem to have lost in the hectic rush of daily living. We can regain the tranquility that we may have possessed as a child or that we know from certain rare moments. We can consciously re-enter those moments of leisure and relaxation by making it a point to integrate them into our daily timetable. We may find ourselves being creative in such a state of calmness and relaxation, and afterward it may seem to us that the solutions occurred on their own without any contribution from us. But in order to enter this special state in which solutions are possible and become obvious to the consciousness, we must first make friends with our unconscious.

The unconscious is the level where creative solutions occur. This is the realm of the id, the source of psychic energy derived from instinctual needs and desires. We can gain access to this level by means of a special form of trance, which you previously might not have considered to be a trance at all. This is the condition in which we are very relaxed, slightly absentminded and dreamy, and not as "with it" as we usually are—in other words, a state in which we are not in the "normal" state of wakefulness. Although we are awake, we are in a soft mood and feel more flowing than usual. We don't want to force or prove anything. This is the best breeding ground for creativity.

Creative Trance Principles

✧ Energy is formed by seemingly unintentional actions.

✧ Tracks are laid down, and new possibilities result. Sense, meaning, benefits, and values don't show themselves until after the trance.

✧ During a creative trance, no calculation or evaluation whatsoever is asked for; that's why this process is called trance and not planning, project building, or consulting.

✧ The unconscious receives an order, which must be expressed precisely.

✧ Dealing with this condition in a playful way has an effect on success.

✧ The play precedes the successful action.

✧ Creativity is never a symbolic or a conceptual process but occurs directly. You can feel it immediately as a physical sensation, an emotional attitude, or a state of mind.

✧ The physical sensation is one of fertility and continuity.

✧ The emotional attitude is one of light euphoria, of being absorbed in yourself, and of complete devotion.

✧ The state of mind shows itself by a paradoxical combination of wakefulness and presence, on the one hand, and a relaxed, nearly indifferent acceptance of what is happening just now, on the other hand. The will of the ego is switched off or remains in the background, and direct contact is made with the unconscious even though you are fully conscious.

✧ The unconscious is the source upon which you can draw during creative processes.

✧ The unconscious has several layers: The upper layer is that of the personal unconscious, the layer below that is the collective unconscious, and an even deeper layer is what is called the ecological self, which contains humankind's archaic experiences. The more direct and the deeper the contact with the unconscious, the more fruitful are the results of the creative process.

✧ Even the best creative process has its limits, and every creative trance has its end. Don't overtax yourself, and set a framework within which you have a scope for your creativity. Respect your infertile phases, when you are dormant, as well as your phases of preparation, or incubation, when you are getting ready for something new, which cannot yet show itself.

✧ Always begin a closure to your creative trance with a feeling of gratitude, regardless of the results of the trance.

✧ Never enter a creative trance under pressure to do well.

✧ Always pay attention to the flow of your breathing, letting it become calm and deep. This way, even under the normal stresses of daily living, you will be able to succeed more and more in inducing a creative mini-trance simply by taking a few deep breaths.

The Visual Creative Trance of Doodling

Under no circumstances should this trance last longer than two hours, and it is even effective in short spurts of time lasting from 10 to 30 minutes. The quicker you put the improvised product on paper, the greater is your chance of entering a true trance state and making contact with your unconscious.

Find a spot where you can sit undisturbed in front of a table. You will need a supply of paper; the best kind for the job is a roll of white paper, which you can tear off in large sheets as needed. For drawing, use soft wax crayons, charcoal, or finger paints. Your materials should not be too expensive to buy, so that you don't have to think about the costs while you are using them.

Your sitting position should be comfortable while also supporting you in an upright position, so that the flow of breath along the vertical axis can mediate between the upper and the lower parts of your body. Also, remember to wear comfortable, warm clothing. Nothing should constrain or distract you, while you start to let the crayon in your hand or your fingers dipped in paint move over the paper.

All your attention is fixed on the unintentional movement of the crayon or your fingers. You are completely in touch with yourself, with the rhythm of your breathing, with the flowing forms that start to take shape on the paper, which then may mix with one another. If you have the feeling that the sheet of paper in front of you is full, take a new one. You can also take a new piece of paper after drawing one line, or draw on top of the forms again and again. It just depends on how complete you are feeling the task is, and on your need for a new beginning. Draw or paint for as long as you feel the inner urge to express yourself. Don't try to show contents, but rather let forms take shape of their own accord. Try to let go of your conscious will and find an attitude in which you feel surprised, moved, and rewarded. All you do is execute the movement with your hand; the real creative act happens by itself, and you let it happen.

When you have completed such a series, you will feel that it is finished. Don't force yourself to demand more from your unconscious. Don't force anything—you will only feel frustrated. Let the end, too, arrive on its own.

Treat the products of your creative trance with respect. This doesn't meant that you have to keep everything you ever produced. But imagine every sheet of paper to be a gift that you received from somewhere, and let yourself feel the energy you have invested in it. If you then want to throw it away, that's fine; it will make space for something new. However, you should never forget that the products don't "just come" but are the results of special efforts. Learn to respect these efforts and to treat them with care.

It's important not to show what you have created indiscriminately to all kinds of people. Without understanding the meaning of the process, they could criticize what they see and destroy your experience.

Look at the pictures that hold a meaning for you. Hang them on the wall, or put them somewhere else where you can look at them often. Because this technique is not just a personal way of expressing yourself, you will be surprised at how often the pictures will give you answers to questions that go beyond the realm of the personal.

The Auditory Creative Trance of Babbling

This trance technique was originally practiced by the whirling dervishes. It is a good idea to do it in a mixed group of beginners and people who know the technique already. This will help break down the initial inhibitions that a lot of people have when it comes to working with their own voice. It is also helpful to play cassettes of other gibberish improvisations that have been recorded to get people going. Then it will become immediately obvious that the babble of voices is not particularly meant to be an aesthetic creation.

As an introduction and a warm-up, you can spend some time just breathing audibly, and then you can start to hum, and finally to speak in single syllables. The syllables can also be sung, declared, called out, or whispered. The syllables can even form words, and the words can frame sentences. The syllables can be left to stand alone, as well, like fragments of an unknown foreign language. As incredible as it seems, during this kind of trance people have even been known to talk fluently in a language previously unknown to them.

You will realize very quickly that vocal expressions can become independent if you allow them to. Suddenly a voice speaks out of you; it is as if one part of yourself can listen to another part speaking out. You may observe that the different voices that emerge from you correspond to certain personalities and characters. Or a whole series of fairy tales can pour out of you, once you have overcome your initial inhibitions and can experience the storytelling as a synchronized translation of silent stories being told at that moment. You don't have to make any contribution. You only have to supply your voice, and the expression follows on its own.

For many people, this feels as if they were being submerged into a sea of meanings and acting as little more than a channel for the retelling of a tale. Incidentally, this trance can be a suitable start into the art of fortune-telling, which actually has more to do with an intuitive understanding of the present than with predicting the future.

Of course, you can do this technique by yourself, especially if you are comfortable with getting started. Try recording what you say in the trance on tape and listening to it later. You may be surprised at how strange your voice sounds to you. At the same time, you may find that something sounds reassuring in it, and that just by listening to it you will go back into the trance state.

Sentences with a positive content that are spoken in your own relaxed "trance voice" naturally have a much greater effect than if you listen to a prerecorded tape with positive affirmations. So, to top off your babbling, try recording certain sentences that have positive effects on you and listening to them when you are relaxed—for example, during your lunch break or before you go to bed. These times of leisure when you are listening to positive statements in your own voice will not only refresh you, but they will also put you in even deeper contact with the wisdom of the self.

The Kinesthetic Creative Trance— a Search for Vision

This type of trance can take many forms: It can be a movement improvisation done to music or performed in absolute silence, a movement therapy session, or even a journey around the world. What is important is the orientation of the search and the motive to start moving.

The motive is this: I want to find something. But what? This doesn't need to be fixed and clear from the beginning. During this search for vision, the objective becomes clearer, step by step. The orientation is strangely paradoxical: On the one hand, I don't know what I'm going to find, but, on the other hand, I assume that what I find is going to be what I have been looking for all along.

You may already have a sense of what you are seeking. It is also possible that, for whatever reason, you don't want to know what could be important in your life right now, and so this is not the time to start a search for vision. But if you feel a combination of openness, expectation, and curiosity regarding where you are heading, then this would be a favorable time for such a journey. An important factor in this quest is having an interest in what is essential. You may be at a crossroads in your life, or you may be in the middle of a crisis or may have just gotten over one, and are now ready to start anew. Perhaps drastic external events have marked your life up to this point, and now you want to take the first steps in actively determining what transpires in the future. In this case, the first steps would be an experience of movement in your search for vision.

Although the word "vision" indicates something visual, the search for vision is only marked to a small extent by visual impressions. The most important element is that of movement, of dynamics. This quest can be a process, a procedure, or even a procession.

As one example, let's take a movement improvisation that you can do at home alone. Find an empty room where you won't be disturbed, and allow yourself a certain amount of time that you can completely devote to your search for vision. Begin by choosing a starting position after trying out different alternatives, such as lying down, crouching, or standing. From this position, you now start to move slowly and, if possible, with your eyes closed, in order to concentrate fully on the inner changes taking place, as well as on your balance, your position, the rhythm that may arise, and the speed that you may gain. Soon you will realize that certain movement patterns are starting to lead you. It may be a swaying motion that has been waiting to express itself, a stretching, or a bobbing from side to side. Allow yourself to be led by your body and its desire for movement; just follow the needs that your body feels moment to moment and wants to express spontaneously. Allow the impulses to come, whatever they might be and however ridiculous they may seem. Make gestures with your hands and fingers, and try different postures.

It's best to keep your eyes closed the entire time, so as to get into better contact with the inner force that is moving you. Remove yourself completely from the outside world, and forget about your self-image, the reflection that you see in the mirror. Travel to your inner self, where you can experience yourself from your core. The first vision that many people have when they start this search has to do with a change in their sense of self. Your sense of your own worth can feel quite different when experienced from the inside as opposed to being judged from the outside. The constant judgment, evaluation, and appraisal in the outside world leads all too often

to a restricted sense of self, which excludes the depths and the breadth of the self and neglects its essence.

If the transition from the outside to the inside is difficult for you, it might be a good idea to do this movement improvisation at first with a group. The exchange afterward can reinforce your own experiences. But it is important that the people involved avoid any evaluation, any analytical or psychological interpretation, any labeling, but limit themselves to observation alone.

Further support can be provided by a piece of music that accompanies and guides you through the trance. The music should last as long as you need for your vision search. These days, there are many pieces of music on tape or CD about a half an hour in length that are designed especially for trances or meditation. The music should be regular, almost monotonous in character, and not composed according to the principles of artistic arrangement, as is a symphony. However, it is preferable to do without any artificial stimulus whatsoever, and to carry out the search for vision some place quiet, like the open countryside.

Once you have become familiar with this form of search within yourself, you can start to write down your observations of your experiences. Then, as time goes by, you will build up a diary containing many vision searches. But take care that you retain an open attitude and don't force the visions into a straightjacket of your personal expectations.

Types of Trance Induction

Let's begin with an assertion: The ways into trance become shorter and shorter.

When I started to induce trances in groups and courses, I asked everyone to repeat simple movements, such as stepping from one leg to the other, swaying up and down, or rocking back and forth, all to the beat of a monotonous drum rhythm. At first, it took a long time to reduce the initial shyness and inhibitions, the reservations, the physical blocks, the tensions of daily living, and the fixed expectations. At the beginning, the room felt cool, sometimes even frosty, and people stood well apart from one another. I asked myself how it would ever be possible for a pleasant atmosphere to arise, for the participants to begin to relate to themselves, to one another, and to me as their teacher. But I knew that by the end of the course, relationships would have developed and that a positive atmosphere would have taken hold of everyone. I could be sure that the trance induction that I offered through dancing and drumming would take effect. It was like a special meal that had to cook for a long time in order to become a success.

Originally, I taught African dance. I came across trance states more or less by chance. My students always liked doing one thing and invariably wanted to do a single thing and more of it, which means they adopted monoideism and monotony instinctively, which, as discussed earlier, are the principles of traditional hypnotherapy. Almost as a secondary result, they found themselves slipping into the pleasant, dreamy state of timelessness. The complicated steps and rhythms of African dance didn't really interest them very much, but in this dreamlike, absent-minded state they mastered them in a playful way. What I discovered from my students' experience is that conditions of pleasant relaxation and trust are prerequisites for successful learning, and that they constitute an art that lies outside of our free will.

Trance dance therapy was imported from Brazil to Europe. When I was first exposed to it with Jacques Donnar, I knew immediately that I had really been teaching this technique all along. Because Donnar had no ambitions with regard to dancing but was more interested in therapy, the purpose was not to learn and master certain movements; instead, free dancing was the focus of the activity. To the accompaniment of deafening drum music, the participants jumped into the circle formed by the group and yielded to their movements, once Donnar had put them into a trance with a turning motion of their necks. These sessions could last for many hours, until everyone had the chance to experience the trance in the middle of the circle.

The group was asked to be attentive to the process, and had to be on the alert for hours in case someone lost his or her balance and fell down or collided with somebody else. But, of course, the main responsibility lay with the therapist or the group leader.

For some years, I worked with this method, which is quite compelling and effective. But eventually I gave it up; working with trance dance is exhausting.

Later I met Felicitas Goodman, whose method of trance induction involved using pumpkin rattles for 15 minutes. In response to all my objections that 15 minutes wasn't long enough, she insisted that the consciousness didn't need any longer to adapt itself to trance and start the inner journey. She explained that experiments had shown that after a longer time, the visions and messages started to repeat themselves, and that dreams, too, conveyed an incredible amount of information in a very short time; moreover, she added, many messages were forgotten anyway, because we can't deal with so much information at one time. She stressed again and again that neither a lot of time or energy was necessary to adapt the organism to trance.

Then I recalled the trance dances in Brazil, which took only one single beat of the holy drums to put the dancers into trance. Even at that time, I doubted that the beat of the drum itself induced the trance. I had the sense that the drumbeat was more like a signal that introduced the trance, and from that point on everyone was in trance because they allowed themselves to be. I raised these questions with ethnologists and anthropologists on a number of occasions, and some agreed with me, whereas others insisted that the body itself needed the appropriate stimulation to be put into a state of readiness for trance.

I observed the trance medium Varda Hasselmann during many of her sessions, and in the process I noticed a series of steps or mini-rituals that repeated themselves. First Varda held her palms in front of her face and deeply inhaled a certain scent from a aura-soma bottle. In this way, she built up a protective barrier between herself and the audience. Then with her eyes closed, she loosened up her neck, as her partner, who was leading her into hypnosis, instructed her to breathe deeply. After a while, instead of further instructions, her partner uttered a single word. The tension in the room increased. I asked what the word meant, and my assumptions were confirmed that it was the name of the great English mystic William Blake. Shortly after that, Varda announced, "I'm ready." Whenever I heard this name afterward, it brought up in me the physical sensation of having arrived in trance. Once I asked Varda why she had chosen Blake, and she told me that, for

her, it brought together in the form of a key word all the trance experiences that she had had in years of training.

During the process of developing my own trance-induction methods, I discovered that we can travel very fast by visualizing light. Therefore, all the time journeys that I offered as a trance induction had elements of being transported on rays of light, which I equated with traveling at the speed of light. In science fiction, this is called "beaming." It is amazing how much faster you can proceed and penetrate areas that are otherwise impenetrable by making use of the power of light, which not only can shine on things but through them as well. That's why I suggested to the participants during a certain trance induction that they possessed a laser beam and had X-ray eyes. The effects were overwhelming.

Now I no longer work with people standing up, but rather with them sitting or lying down. I discovered that movement is only necessary at the beginning and the end of a trance session, in order to find and dissolve the trance condition. I understood this to be so because the body, as a medium of embodiment of our present condition, needs to be accompanied into and out of the changed state. After all, most of the changes that are induced by trance happen inside the body. As an embodiment of psychological processes and mental functions, the body is the only place where changes take place, or where changes that had been thought of and felt before are converted into corresponding new behavior.

The aim of every therapeutic trance is to achieve positive changes and transformations. After the trance, your attitude should change by itself and produce different behavior. All this happens on a physical level. We are aware of this level when we use our bodies consciously—for example, when we are dancing or participating in sports. When practicing the Oriental martial arts, in particular, we go beyond the usual physical level and act on the level of an all-pervading life energy.

The kinesthetic trance—which makes use of movement and touching, both active and passive—is one of the oldest methods for healing, having been used in shamanistic and other archaic cultures. Even today, the kinesthetic trance holds great attraction for many people; yet it is also a source of anxiety, because the kinesthetic memory stores all the prenatal, perinatal, and early childhood experiences that are not accessible to the consciousness.

The body has its own ways of going into trance. The consciousness doesn't need to be switched off, but the essential events unravel on the fully automatic level of behavior control. The ego cannot do anything about it. That's the reason why such "body trances" are mainly used in situations in which the trance takes place against the will of a person—for example, during torture and brainwashing. When such a loss of control happens during a therapeutic trance, it is understandable that deep anxieties arise. The ego stands under the threat of destruction.

This makes sense when we think about how autonomous, automatic survival reactions, with all their reflexes and impulses, relate to the human mind and consciousness. Survival is a pattern developed by evolution that we share with other creatures. Varying from species to species, the pattern always strives to keep the species alive, if only by virtue of reproduction. Human thought, however, takes place in a type of memory where experience has been stored as speech and can be called up again with the help of speech. Human consciousness can change and thereby effect a change in behavior patterns. Changes can also occur without con-

sciousness. Thus, we can decide by means of the type of trance induction we use whether to address the more archaic behavior patterns or whether we want to initiate changes with our consciousness.

Both methods have vehement advocates. Some believe that the essence of trance is just this relinquishing of control and the elimination of the ego. Others insist on the use of free will and the possibility of changes being brought about by the person's own volition. In this case, intelligence and imagination seem to be the determinants for success. Personally, I suspect that the best approach lies somewhere in the middle. Nonetheless, you have to find out for yourself whether you prefer to induce trance in a kinesthetic (instinctive, motor) or in a mental (imaginative) way.

It's important to realize that kinesthetic trances aren't only associated with ideas of fear and being overwhelmed, but also with expectations of adventure and fun.

The kinesthetic sense has to do with motion, but also with touch, balance, and contact. In Western society, adults don't make much use of this sense in everyday living, although the types of trance induction with which we are most familiar address this sense. Certain fairground rides involving spinning and speed fall into this category. Dancing until the person is almost in a hypnotic state, as practiced in the days of acid rock and now at techno-discos, is reminiscent of the St. Vitus dances of the Middle Ages or of the shaking or shivering trances of charismatic sects, such as the Shakers (who took their name from such trances). In our body-hostile culture, the physical release achieved here is in itself an act of crossing boundaries and moving on to unfamiliar or even extraordinary terrain; it represents a kind of excessiveness that may not be so unusual in other cultures where the physical level is more of an accepted part of life.

What is true for ecstatic movement applies even more to the experience of touch. Simply being part of a large crowd of people can induce a trance that doesn't necessarily need to manifest the negative traits of mass hysteria. I witnessed spontaneous healing in California at an international meeting of spirit healers that was part of a mass event. Many of those present said that it was the energy of everyone there that made the experience so powerful. At that time, I interpreted this as American optimism, but today I see it in a different light.

The healing touch has always been a potent instrument for restoring and maintaining people's health. But this most natural, simple, and inexpensive remedy has such a strong taboo associated with it that in some countries healers are forbidden by law to lay their hands on the patient. The healing trance that ensues from the loving attention of touch calls up an original unity and at the same time satisfies childlike needs, yet it quickly comes under suspicion of representing regression and sexual interference. In fact, the boundaries here may be fluid, which is why it is so important to experience these trances with your own body and to get a clear idea of their suggestive effects before using them on other people.

In hypnotherapy and Neurolinguistic Programming (NLP), the body contact between the therapist and the client is limited to the anchoring of new information and experiences, which are stored in the body and can be called up again at any time by means of slight touching. The touch that causes the effect of remembering and visualizing provides immediate access to everything new you have learned as a result of the differentiating decision-making process during trance. Affirmations are also used to represent anchors, which are "dropped" to ensure

and prolong the effect of the therapy. Used without the therapeutic process, during which affirmations were found to be an effective remedy, they have little meaning; they are sentences whose significance cannot be understood by the logical mind, because they only appeal to the inner authorities that were activated during trance and are responsible for the self-healing process. This is true as well for processes of personal experience and meditation without accompanying psychotherapy, in which we are fully dependent on the strength and the clarity of our own suggestions.

–The shortest trance induction I have experienced to date consisted of just two sentences: "Shining rays of light fill my body. I transport myself into the center of creation, and I do this by just wanting to think it now." In no time at all, I was there, although I couldn't imagine what the center of creation could be. My body, however, recalled at lightning speed all the experiences of trance induction that had brought about changes of consciousness in me, and arrived at a state in which I could answer the questions put to me by my mind with an amazing certainty. In this condition, I experienced myself as being clear and alert. It was a state of heightened concentration, during which I could answer specific questions that would never have come to my mind in my everyday consciousness.

However, in all probability, I would not have been able to experience such alertness within the trance state without having had years of intensive work with trance. My body was well prepared, and all my mind had to do was enter. You could say that I had worked my way up the ladder of the trance hierarchy. I had started with archaic trance induction, which was mainly kinetic (meaning active or dynamic), like the trance dance. And my experiences with Oriental martial arts helped in putting my body in a state of highly energized vibration (the Chi state) and helped me in dealing with such energies.

What is the best way into trance for you?

Would you rather dance for hours on end or be inundated by the sounds of rattles, drums, and gongs? Are drugs indispensable? Do you need the thrill, the rush of adrenaline, that occurs in dangerous situations? Do you need the kick of the endorphins of the body that are released through muscle impulses during activities like jogging? Or is it enough for you to attend a ceremonial ritual together with many other people who are as deeply moved as you are and are even able to show this, because it is a socially acceptable ritual? Do you get transported when you smell incense, or do you feel sick? What happens inside of you when you sit in front of an open fire or gaze into the flickering light of a candle? Do you prefer mantras or the rosary? Is it easiest for you to go into trance when you are lying down in a darkened room, breathing deeply and without pause for an hour or so? Does it have an effect on you when your neighbor starts to groan, having obviously entered a deep cathartic process, or when he or she starts to snore, having fallen asleep? Is it enough just to pray? Can worship be a form of trance? Is it sufficient for you to go to the theater or a concert, where you can be captivated and forget about everything else? What about slips in everyday life, like missing the correct highway exit or going on a spending spree? Are these trances too? Can you also be in trance—and therefore off the hook—when you arrive somewhere late simply because you didn't notice the time?

What is most important to realize is this: Every person is different, so we have different methods and patterns of going into trance. Probably we are far more often in a state of trance than we want to admit.

The first step in the process is to recall altered or unusual states of consciousness, and to describe their particular characteristics. What was so special about these states? What do you remember best? What impressions do you associate with the word "trance"? What physical sensations do you remember from these altered states? Which metaphors would you use to describe these experiences? Soon you will realize what your preferences for trance induction are. You will observe that you use some sensory channels more often than others to maintain control, and that similarly you are more open to suggestions on certain sensory channels than on others.

The second step is to relinquish any fears or doubts regarding your own suggestibility and your ability to go into trance, valuing the experience of trance instead as a gift. This attitude will enable you to use trance consciously. Fear and doubt are conditions in which we feel weak. Realize your weakness, and then ask yourself: Do I want to be weak? You will be surprised to find that you do have a choice. You can turn weakness into strength and make it represent a chance to accept responsibility.

The third step is to create the outer framework that you will need for the inner trance journey. When doing this, you need to consider your own needs and take yourself seriously. Approach this journey from the outset as the possibility of having a valuable, enriching experience. Find a spot where you feel comfortable, warm, and secure. Fix a certain time during which you can become fully involved in the process, making arrangements so that you won't be disturbed either by the doorbell, the telephone, or children. You might create a certain space especially for this purpose. Don't give up, however, the first time there is an interruption. Many times such incidents even represent a welcome break. The important point is this: The decisiveness with which you go into a consciously identified trance will determine the results you will achieve.

Nonetheless, the fourth step involves giving yourself some latitude in order to reduce the pressure of doing well. Don't put yourself under stress! Don't overtax yourself with exaggerated expectations! Pretend that you don't have any expectations at all and are just going through the motions. This can encourage a playful absence of intention, which is exactly right as a basic attitude toward trance, because the more you expect, the quicker the controlled will of your ego will thwart your plans while the id will refuse to obey.

Take it easy, and treat this process like a game. Practice wanting nothing, while at the same time knowing exactly what it is all about. Step by step, you will gain confidence in your abilities and enjoy greater and greater contact with your own self.

In step five, be aware of not confusing your readiness to go into trance with the victim attitude. Don't ever get into a situation in this context in which you feel helpless or at the mercy of some outside force. Never give in to your desire for a sensation that will take you into unknown, threatening, or risky and socially condemned border areas of human consciousness. Save your curiosity for the conscious and responsible use of trance, and establish it as a personal principle to never do anything beneath your dignity and self-respect, not even in trance. Only such a forthright and level attitude will enable you to encounter your own unconscious. And only then will this contact be an enriching experience, which is not disorienting or disintegrating but leads to true integration and integrity.

It's good to have curiosity and a desire for self-awareness, but in step six you are advised not to constantly ask yourself whether or not you are actually in a state of trance. This kind of continual evaluation is the best way to miss new experiences, especially in trance. It is better to ask yourself, once the trance session is over, if the effects were what you had expected from trance. Remember your initial motivation to draw benefits from the state of trance, and use your own goals as criteria. Afterward, also assess to what extent you were able to open up to the experience of trance, to open up to your own self. If you find that you did not go deep enough, don't put the blame on anyone, not even yourself. Instead, use this assessment as a basis for trying to go deeper in the future, in order to get into even closer contact with what will bring you toward your goals of its own accord.

Ways into Trance Through the Senses

Our senses connect us to what we know as reality. How reality takes effect and whether or not it reaches us depend on our senses. The senses are channels through which we receive information. We are constantly picking up new impulses, which, by the time they reach our consciousness, have already been filtered. Only very little information truly comes into the limelight of our attention, where it is recognized as reality and as the truth. Thus, most of the impressions on our senses remain below the threshold of our consciousness and have no substance for us, even though they, too, are part of reality—but only of unconscious reality. We receive messages, not only from our environment but also from the realm of unconscious reality, that reach our consciousness as impulses. The impulses that we receive from the outside world as well as from the inner world can set off both mental conditions and emotional moods and states that seem to emerge out of nowhere. They can also trigger physical sensations—suddenly we feel heavy, lethargic, or tired, without knowing why.

What are the requirements for a perception to be deemed true and conscious in the contents of our consciousness? The most important criterion for this is certainly that of significance. Whatever we consciously perceive has to go through certain processes of preliminary decisions, evaluations, and tests to get to the threshold of consciousness. But these preliminary decisions as to what is important and what isn't are not predetermined but rather depend on our horizon of experience, which in turn is determined by our experiences so far. Thus, the present situation is never viewed in an unbiased and direct manner; on the contrary, we see it as if through a special pair of glasses. Psychoanalysts talk about "projections": The consciousness, which has processed the experiences so far to form a meaningful whole, projects on to the new experience the grids and patterns of the discovery of meaning that has taken place up to now, and thus the new experience reflects all the baggage of the old experiences. What made sense so far is now most likely to make sense again, so it can be said that subjective reality develops from making sense.

The sensory structure, from which the truth is distilled, is determined by the machinations of selection, with perceptions corresponding to certain patterns. It is not only the pattern that you recognize, but also the sensory channel where the information is recorded. Some people don't hear or see very well, without there being a physiological basis to the problem; a sense may be impaired as a result of a psychosomatic reaction, thus sabotaging a person's ability to receive information, because the channel that he or she is receiving it on is blocked by hurtful experiences. According to our character type, there are certain preferences for one sensory channel over another, so it is an advantage to know which type you are in order to be most receptive. Furthermore, the neurotic structures of such psychosomatic reactions as blindness and deafness can be dissolved through greater knowledge about the nature of the senses and the different sensory channels.

Basically, the aim is to have perceptions that are influenced as little as possible by earlier experiences. Of course, these unbiased, direct, and immediate perceptions are the ideal, but they rarely occur in everyday life. In the endeavors of Far Eastern meditation and likewise in the perception exercises of Buddhism, this goal plays an important role. Neurolinguistic Programming (NLP) proceeds along utilitarian lines and orients itself toward the sensory channel that provides the individual with the maximum amount of information. But this functionality, which is practiced, for example, in modern sales training, contains the danger of an individual committing him- or herself too one-sidedly and too early to a particular character type. The result is a certain stereotyped style, which, for a salesperson, may well drive away more clients than that it attracts.

Nevertheless, I have decided to describe the various character types here, because these types have a bearing on which means of trance induction will most likely provide the easiest access to the trance experience for you.

NLP distinguishes between:

❖ the auditory type,

❖ the visual type, and

❖ the kinesthetic type.

The Auditory Type

People in this category are not only adapted to the sensory channel of listening (auditory-tonal type), but they also have a stronger feeling for speech (auditory-digital type). These are the people most likely to be in constant dialogue with themselves, discussing everything. Often they also have an inner commentator who, in the role of a censor, never fails to contribute its own opinion. The inner voice of intuition is blotted out by many other voices, and at the threshold of consciousness the voice of the critic whispers its doubts and reservations. Auditory people like to understand everything exactly, and they often read reference books to comprehend a subject. An experience itself doesn't count as much as their knowledge about it, even if it is secondhand. They read a great deal, but they don't necessarily read quickly and effectively, because they tend to read every word almost under their breath. The overall meaning of a text doesn't immediately become apparent to them, but has to be ascertained step by step or word by word.

The time when the gods spoke to people through inner voices has to be considered a very strenuous and conflict-ridden phase in the history of human consciousness. What we call "intellect" only developed through speech. Intellectuals are often auditory types and are by nature very skeptical about trance. They listen to a spoken trance induction meticulously, wanting to understand every word, doubting the content, and considering what an expression might mean, and they are surprised when they find that they have memory gaps afterward, because they succumbed to the trance or simply fell asleep at the end.

For some auditory types, it is best to make use of a different sense channel to trick the inner censor. Listening to music as a trance induction can be effective, provided that the listener is not a professional musician or a passionate music lover. You can recognize auditory-digital types by their rational attitude: They have stored the whole world in their mind in linguistic formulas. They are often witty in their use of language and have a wide vocabulary. But, at the same time, they are easily beguiled and seduced in areas where they least expect it: through those senses that are either partially or not at all governed by conscious control, such as touch, smell, and taste. In evolutionary terms, these senses are very old, and they still have an effect on the archaic level of the instincts.

The Visual Type

Visual types are able to visualize everything, and they have good access to their own inner pictures. Emotions unroll like an inner movie, and a range of colors, geometric patterns, and flowing designs present themselves to those who look inside. Here, the disadvantage is that the richness of the person's own pictures often blocks access to the depths that lie behind or below the pictures.

Not only are people who fall into this category focused on seeing, but they also take an interest in being seen. Their tendency toward self-expression and stylization fits in with trance, which works with inner pictures and movies and at the same time calls for ceremonial and ritual expression. Many of the traditional trance rites, as they still exist today in incantations, initiation rites, exorcism, and so forth, have festive trappings. Visual types love performances; in fact, they are nothing short of dependent on them, because their own way of experiencing things is so determined by pictures. An "exotic" trance in a folkloric context can put the visual type of person into trance just by watching it. Ethnographic material, too, in the form of photos or films, can have a similar impact; the strength of the picture can be sufficient to put the visual type into a mood receptive to trance.

Modern advertising appeals almost exclusively to the visual type. The general tendency of the transfer of information, or communication, seems to be heading toward giving more and more visual data instead of using speech or physical contact. TV is a collective visual trance induction, especially when the main emphasis is on pictures instead of words. Only very few can resist this trance. Today, there are special trance videos on the market, which have constantly pulsating and flickering patterns, and thereby change one's state of consciousness. In addition, the flickering and flashing of neon signs imprint themselves on the mind; in fact, everything shiny or glittery (even glossy paper) addresses the visual sense and has the capacity to cast a spell.

The Kinesthetic Type

This character type requires physical experiences. As far as trance induction goes, all kinds of physical activities can be effective. In early morning jogging or professional or amateur sports, the aim is to improve on one's previous performance and exceed the limits of one's own capacity. When learning a certain technique, it is always the body that moves step by step into extraordinary conditions and thus processes, stores, and can call up again the learning experiences. Suddenly a specific jump, dance step, turn, or stroke works as if by magic. The id takes the lead, while the ego watches in surprise. Naturally, in this form of kinesthetic learning, it is possible and even desirable for other senses to also make a contribution. Thus, the movement leading into trance may be accompanied by supporting words or stimulating music, and the teacher may demonstrate the movement and make the quality of the movement easier to understand through his or her own example.

The kinesthetic type also likes to be addressed by touch. A massage can put a person into a changed state of consciousness. Healing by touch can induce trance as well. Physical contact with a partner in small or large groups is another good way of switching off the intellect. For people inexperienced in trance, kinesthetic trance induction is especially recommended to reduce anxieties and doubts, because it is supported by their own physical experiences.

Their own well-being is the decisive factor for kinesthetic types. They want to experience the personal benefit of their efforts; therefore, this is the yardstick by which they measure the value of a certain means of trance induction. You can often recognize people in this category by the comfortable clothing they wear, which, like a second skin, gives them the appearance of being at ease, secure, and familiar. For these people, their own depth and inwardness is easily accessible when they are in a condition of personal well-being. Extreme distortions of balance or other dramatic disturbances, as can occur during ecstatic conditions, impair the pleasure they take in the extraordinary. Therefore, the kinesthetic trance induction has to be carefully built up and proper attention must be paid to the consequences.

Gaining Access to the Supersensory

The transition from the sensory to the supersensory takes place through the finer perception of what no longer exists materially as a "coarse cloth" but expresses itself as energy and vibrations on a "finely woven" level. If you work a great deal with trance, you will find that not only will your perceptions become finer and finer and that you will become more and more sensitive, but that you will also develop an increasingly greater feeling for the supersensory, which our normal senses can no longer perceive, because they have degenerated over the course of civilization. The refinement that leads into supersensory reality affects all five senses. Therefore, you not only will hear and see more clearly, but your senses of taste, touch, and smell will also become more developed.

Later in this chapter, types of trance induction for all five senses will be discussed. Every sense is assigned to a particular chakra, which has proven to be very effective, because in this way each sense can be "attached" to a certain energy level and be more easily recognized in its functions. Furthermore, through the chakras, we are better able to perceive and differentiate energies. This is because a chakra is a center of energy in the "finely woven material," meaning in the energetic body of a person, which is connected by the nerve network in that part of the body to the "coarsely woven material," or the palpable body.

The chakras can also be regarded as organs of perception, for they take up very high and fast impulses of an energy field as vibrations and translate them into more physically agreeable and "coarser," meaning lower, vibrations. On this level, sensory impressions make sense and can be understood. However, if they are not switched over, they mostly remain below the perception level and are not noticed by the consciousness. Therefore, trance also has to do with an increase of physical vibrations, in order to gain access to those areas of the supersensory that are characterized by fast and high-pitched vibrations.

Before going into the types of trance induction that make use of the different senses, we will discuss breathing as a way into trance, because breathing techniques have been shown to provide an excellent access to all the other methods of trance induction.

Trance Induction Through Breathing

In the West, the German word *atmen*, to breathe, is related to the old Indian Sanskrit word *atman*, meaning breath or soul. According to the Jewish/Christian myth of creation, God formed man after His image and breathed life into him. Breath is connected to being alive but also to spirituality. The Latin word *spiritus* means breath as well as spirit. Therefore, it is not surprising that breathing techniques are part of many methods of trance induction, because they change not only a person's spiritual and mental attitudes but also the chemistry of one's body. The whole organism is affected. Breathing is described in many ways, and we use a number of metaphors related to breath.

Breathing can be slow or fast, weak or strong, short or long, deep or shallow; it can be panting, whistling, wheezing, or rattling. Breath can stand still, get caught, or simply stop; it can also come in gulps or puffs. We take a breath, or draw a breath; fear presses in on breathing or cuts it off. Sometimes breathing, which usually occurs of its own accord, seems to be very difficult, and we are fighting for our breath. Reading this, you may find yourself imagining a corresponding situation or remembering an experience you have had. How do you feel when you are short of breath? What does heaving a sigh of relief, and breathing freely and deeply, feel like? When, during the normal course of a day, do you find yourself breathing in one way or another?

Now, read the metaphors connected to breath that follow and let them sink in, *feeling* what they have to tell you: Something takes your breath away; you are told not to breathe a word; you are awestruck, or breathless; something happens, and you can now breathe freely; you watch with bated breath; when something will take a while, you are told not to hold your breath. There are also phrases like heavy breathing and a breathless silence.

Breathing techniques for trance induction have a long history, and are still used today with great success, especially before using other means of trance induction. Unlike some other methods for going into trance, they don't cost a cent and are legal. You need no special equipment and no preparation, except locating a quiet spot and giving yourself plenty of time.

Exercise: Breathing Deeply

It is a sign of our hectic times that people take very little or no time at all for themselves. That's why people often have short and flat breath nowadays. The best remedy for this is the simple decision to breathe deeply more often. It works wonders!

By breathing deeply, you take a break from the gray monotony of everyday life, and soon find that you have added more color to it. Breathing can make you euphoric! Let more euphoria flow into your life by granting yourself more oxygen, which is a basic foodstuff needed by your organism and especially your brain. Particularly in situations that are difficult or even seem hopeless, it is all the more important that you don't hold your breath but let it flow. Take deep breaths before you tackle a difficult task—don't go into battle with a defeatist attitude!

Exercise: Breathing Out Fully and Letting Go

Make it a rule to pay attention more often to how your breath flows. You will probably discover that you hold your breath to varying degrees more often than you would have thought. You may even realize that sometimes not only do you hold your breath but also swallow it. This is a sign of nervousness and leads to a feeling of being bloated, or inflated, inside. Especially if we eat quickly, we often swallow air while gobbling down the food. The custom of saying grace at meals has, among others, the aim of making us forget our worries for a while and concentrate on the present. Although praying is a request, it also provides space for feelings of gratitude and respect. These feelings create an inner space, allowing the breath to flow in a different way from when we feel greed, envy, jealousy, ambition, or dislike. So, breathe out fully before you take a bite of food. Make yourself available and free to take in new things. Then you will also be able to digest food better.

Of course, you can practice breathing on other occasions besides when you are eating. Whenever you want to adjust completely to the present, breathe out consciously and deeply. Do this, for example, before you start talking or as you enter a room for a business appointment. Allow yourself to become empty, in order to accept and enjoy a new fullness.

Breathing out is also a good antidote to the negative spell of fear, which is restricting. However, before you breathe against it by trying to fight it desperately by breathing in, breathe out first. Go *with* the fear, not against it. Empty yourself so that there is nowhere for fear to take hold. If it cannot gain a foothold, it flows away. With the act of breathing out, the fear is released as well.

Breathing out can eliminate anything old, superfluous, poisonous, or laborious, anything you want to let go of. Imagine how everything that you don't need anymore leaves you when you breathe out. In some trance techniques, exhalation is specifically used to carry out an inner cleansing process. We can imagine the breath as black smoke that enters the cosmic cycle of transformation in a way that is similar to nitrogen. For humans, this black smoke is poison, whereas, for plants, it is important nourishment, just as the oxygen that the plants release means nourishment for us.

By imagining a large cosmic recycling center, I'm motivated to let go of my waste (breath), because I know that something else will benefit from it. But if I still have pangs of conscience and hold on, I will reduce myself to a refuse chute and do harm to my health. To get around this, in another trance technique the breath that is exhaled is visualized as black; then it cleans itself, and can be breathed back in as a white substance.

Exercise: Breathing Out with Expression, and In with Inspiration

In the martial arts, activity is always placed in the phases of prolonged and controlled breathing out. If the adversary is taken by surprise during the regenerating phase of breathing in, this is an advantage, because the organism, which first has to take a deep breath, is so occupied with itself and turned to the inside that it has no strength left over for the outside. During a fight, this is a weakness. In a different situation—for example, during regeneration or a creative pause—this weakness becomes a strength. It depends on the situation and the related task.

Breathing out is associated with activity, expression, and effect. Inspiration, however, as the word itself indicates, is connected to breathing in. Pay attention to your own breath in phases of activity or expression and when you turn inward for regeneration or inspiration.

Exercise: Counting Breaths

This is an excellent preparation exercise before a trance induction. It makes you feel calm and composed, and it distracts you from your inner monologue. It's difficult to have a stimulating inner discussion while breathing evenly and calmly. Most of the time, we are compulsively preoccupied with inner discussions, constantly commenting and justifying. However, if we want to pause, we first have to offer the restless mind a substitute to occupy it and calm it down.

The counting process is great for this, because it has no content and is only form. If you count to three while breathing in, and to five while breathing out, counting to four in each pause between breathing out and breathing in and counting to one between breathing in and breathing out, then your consciousness is occupied with ordering the process of breathing. There is nothing the consciousness likes more; it finally has something to do! This counting exercise has a peaceful effect and conveys a feeling of order. Now your attention can turn from the outside to the inside, and you are ready for the trance journey.

Exercise: Chaotic Breathing

Another technique you can use to interrupt the inner monologue before going into trance is that of chaotic breathing. Contrary to even, rhythmic breathing, in this case the breath adapts to the speed and rhythm of a piece music or drumming that is full of unexpected changes. The consciousness cannot get used to a rhythm of breathing, but instead has to readapt all the time. Because thinking and conscious breathing are difficult if not impossible to do simultaneously, the pattern of the inner monologue is broken.

Exercise: Breathing In and Experiencing Ecstasy

Consciously take in the energy of life; attract it and absorb it, suck it in, and feed on it! In many courses on breath training, it is asserted repeatedly that breathing in happens of its own accord. And that's true. But if I want to get carried away—and who doesn't want to do this at times?—then I will want to draw in air as a valuable gift, to let it fill me, pump me up, make me feel high or intoxicated. If I breathe in deeply or quickly for a while, this can produce a tickling in my head and a flickering in front of my eyes, making me feel almost as if I had taken drugs. But here we are dealing with the body's own drugs, to which no real objection can be raised.

We speak of a "jogger's high," for example, which takes effect, without marihuana or cocaine, when we get our second wind in the physical strain of running. Jogging, in fact, is often used during withdrawal therapies as a means of replacing an artificial high with a self-produced one. The disadvantage here is that we have to run longer and longer in order to persuade the organism to produce the body's own drugs. And this can become a problem, because in the end we will be spending all our time running!

Of course, in cases of addiction, the structure of the addition has to be worked on with psychotherapy. Nonetheless, trance techniques in general and especially those employing breathing are well suited to withdrawal therapy. This is true not only for drug addiction but also for addiction to other poisons, like nicotine and alcohol, and for addictive behavior, as seen in compulsive gamblers and workaholics. The addiction is satisfied by ecstatic states produced within our own bodies. Ecstasy is part of life, also part of modern living. So, it is good to know that by using a very simple breathing method, we can make contact with our ecstatic potential.

Exercise: Conscious Hyperventilation

When some fright makes you breathe quite rapidly and thus pumps too much oxygen into your brain, this can create a condition of hyperventilation, which can feel very unpleasant and even produce a feeling of panic. The panic is often accompanied by cramps and stiffness, which increase it further. But if you are doing a technique involving conscious and deliberate hyperventilation (for example, "rebirthing"), then you don't try to stop hyperventilating out of fear, but instead succumb to the organic flow of the rapid breathing. Now, rather than causing panic, the tension created relaxes the body, and you are soon filled with a *joie de vivre* far greater than normal.

Exercise: Holding the Breath to Give a Signal

This is an advanced trance-induction technique, although children have been known to practice it. Perhaps you remember as a child being proud of how long you could stay under water holding your breath. You may have even mastered this to the extent that you turned blue in the face, giving your parents such a shock that they finally gave you the attention you had been craving all along. But if this occurred, you may not remember it anymore, because it probably happened some time in early childhood, when neither consciousness nor speech had fully developed. Children are very good at catapulting themselves into states of emergency, either out of the fun of the adventure, as a test of courage and proof of their own bravery, or as a clever blackmail maneuver. In any event, holding one's breath is something that goes back to early childhood and is also a magical technique dating back to ancient times.

In some visualization techniques, in which the aim is to fulfil our innermost wishes, we hold in our breath to give the body this signal: Hey, wake up, something remarkable is going to begin right now, so pay attention! When the organism has registered the signal, then all the body's protection mechanisms and defense systems are put on the alert, attention is concentrated, and everything is tensed up.

If you now feed in the picture of your wishes like a slide and project it onto the empty, receptive screen of your consciousness, then you can be sure of undivided attention. Everything within you concentrates on the picture, as if it was branded on your forehead. It is a program that you install and store yourself, an image that you carve into your consciousness.

Eliminating such a suggestion burned into the brain is not easy to do, so think about this carefully before you do it. Once you have written on the banner and put it in place, it's hard to take it down again, and it can sometimes act as a straitjacket. As long as you carry such a banner around with you, the delicious breeze of freedom can no longer reach you so easily. So, think about whether having your wishes fulfilled are worth this sacrifice.

Exercise: Exhaling—Letting Go, Entering Emptiness, Dying

Each time you breathe out offers you a small foretaste of dying, just as every time you breathe in can be like being reborn. To consciously let the process of breathing out pass into a phase of emptiness and quiet is a good preparation for meditative trances. These allow you to experience dying as a part of living and to gain access to the other side. Here, what you experience is the opposite of the hectic activity of daily living, although it is still part of the rhythm of life, which alternates between the poles of engaging in action and letting things happen, of giving and taking, of transmitting and receiving. This technique is especially suitable for learning to be a better listener. Close your eyes, let your eyeballs drop, breathe out, and stay like this for a while, as if time had stopped. Now you are completely tuned in to receive, and you allow everything to come that wants to come.

Exercise: Circular Breathing

Another trance-induction technique that is governed by the controlled flow of breath is circular breathing, which combines breathing in and breathing out, with the smooth transition of one to the other creating a cycle. This can happen in three different ways:

✧ Slow circular breathing, in which the breathing in is done audibly through the slightly opened mouth and the breathing out also happens audibly through the mouth. You can imagine making the sound of the wind or even a wild storm when doing this. As an alternative, you can breathe out through the nose (wheezing or puffing).

✧ Medium-fast circular breathing, in which the mouth remains shut and the breath moves audibly in and out through the nose (sniffing).

✧ Fast circular breathing, or panting. Should too much oxygen get to the brain, you may feel a tickling in your hands and pressure in your head. You can compensate for this by breathing out emphatically and fully.

Exercise: Combining Breathing with the Different Senses

✧ Breathe in while looking at an object that you want to bring closer and internalize.

✧ Breathe out while looking at an object that you want to keep at a distance or push away.

You can do the same thing with the other senses. Breathing in moves things closer; breathing out moves things away.

Exercise: Chakra Breathing

✧ First chakra—Smelling

✧ Second chakra—Tasting

✧ Third chakra—Looking

✧ Fourth chakra—Feeling

✧ Fifth chakra—Listening

✧ (Sixth and seventh chakras—no classification)

With the following trance-induction techniques, which are assigned to one or another of the five senses, you can move the trances to the relevant body areas of the chakras through consciously controlled breathing.

Trance Induction Through the Sense of Smell

The sense of smell is assigned to the first chakra, and it has something to do with our ability to orient ourselves instinctively in the world. It functions even when all the other senses are not operating, which is why, in the days when women were given to frequent fainting spells, they always carried smelling salts with them. Smells transmit direct information that enters the consciousness primarily when something is wrong. Then the wakeful consciousness, which takes care of our safety, tries to find out what the problem is. However, most of the time, the consciousness doesn't have the foggiest idea. Over the years of human evolution, our sense of smell has dulled. We tend not to notice pleasant smells very much at first, so they influence our state of well-being positively but largely unconsciously. For example, if the air is especially clean and fresh, we may find ourselves taking deep, relishing breaths, yet not being particularly aware of the smell of the air itself.

Artificial scents overlay body odors, which in the past were considered to be erotic.

Interestingly, the word "smell" is used in its intransitive as well as its transitive form: Somebody smells (intransitive—connoting smelling badly or even stinking), and somebody smells something (transitive use). So, smell is something that is given off and also taken in.

Certain smells relate to memories, and call them forth into the present as a complex structure of numerous perceptions. Nothing can fix an experience so strongly and indelibly in our memories as a smell to which we are conditioned. Perhaps from your own experience the smell of floor wax, for example, awakens the memory of classrooms and thus brings whole periods of your school days back to life. Or certain smells in staircases or stations may be connected to various periods of time and different countries. What are especially exciting for me when I am traveling are the strange smells through which I take in everything exotic.

Various expressions in language remind us that smelling in an active sense shows a certain ability—namely, that of an instinctive, earthy, and sensory intelligence (like native cunning). Think about these expressions: to have a nose for something, to be on the nose, to have a good nose, to be ahead by a nose. At the same time, there are expressions that are less flattering or appealing, like taking up a scent like a tracker dog, smelling a rat, nosing into something, and sniffing something out. In the past in certain cultures, a broad nose with large nostrils was considered to be a sign of being dominated by physical urges, and didn't conform to the ideal of beauty of a demure girl.

In connection with trance induction, smelling plays an important role in both the active and the passive sense. Especially when you wish to address the unconscious, you should take special care to ensure that the smell of the room is agreeable. Burning incense has always been used to prepare and purify a ritual room where a trance was to be induced. The smoke has a cleansing effect, especially when it comes from certain herbs, such as sage. Other aromas have an effect on the conscience, like the incense that was still used in the Catholic mass up to the Second Vatican Council. The intellectual Beat scene of the fifties was associated with the smells of cigarettes, red wine, and marihuana, which later became the hallmarks of the freewheeling hippie lifestyle of the sixties and the seventies. The eighties saw the arrival of scent lamps, which filled the air with the aromas of essential oils. Today, the trend continues with a preference for scents taken from nature. As supersen-

sory people always tell me, artificial scents make the aura shrink and collapse like a soufflé. Nevertheless, anyone who is reasonably aware has to admit that synthetic scents seem rather stale and pale in comparison with those of essential oils. Aromas not only affect what we might call the "coarsely woven material" body of a person but also penetrate to the finest spheres of energetic relations. Smells can be either nourishment or poison for the aura.

The body odor of a person changes with his or her physical, emotional, and mental state. Illness and mental disturbances, as well as being overwhelmed by strong feelings, can express themselves through smells that are discharged. In the past, it was said that the saints smelled of roses.

In early times, smoke signals were known as a form of ritual contact with the gods and spirits, and had a particular meaning during sacrificial rites. Cain slew Abel because the smoke from his own sacrifice did not ascend heavenward as straight as his brother's did. Murder from smoke envy! Smoke creates a sign that can be seen from afar—like a house on fire, for instance. Smoke also points to something; as the proverb says, "Where there's smoke, there's fire." Smoking together unites people, and is used as a communication ritual on both ordinary and festive occasions; take, for example, the sharing of the peace pipe by Native Americans, for whom smoking marihuana is a religious ritual. "Smudging" (cleansing by burning) is another Native American ritual.

However, in the West, methods of trance induction involving smelling, burning, or smoking generally play a less important role than they do elsewhere. But this may change if it becomes socially more acceptable to have a keen sense of smell—like an acute sense of hearing, for example.

A trance can be induced by a pleasant aroma triggering spontaneous deep breathing. When using scents, we have to differentiate between stimulating and calming aromas—ones that support concentration and mental tension and are suitable for learning situations, and ones that invite us to relax and have an erotic effect. It's important to choose the appropriate scent, depending on the goal of your trance or autosuggestion. If you are working with a group, remember to test the scent beforehand and not only on yourself. In any case, the scent shouldn't be too unusual, shouldn't be pungent, and should be used discreetly. Certain scents may be satisfactory but can still call up unpleasant memories; for example, bergamot may remind some people of school floors polished with floor wax, and thus evoke in them associations having to do with the stress and the pressure of school and with sweating over exams.

Breathing techniques to induce trance can be strengthened by imagining deeply breathing in a pleasant aroma, such as the scent of a rose. Fast breathing, as is used in rebirthing, can be supported by picturing a curious and excited hunting dog. New things will become accessible by sniffing on an instinctive level, with curiosity emerging as a sensory experience, which is a very effective means in itself of combating resignation!

Smells that are associated with certain pleasant incidents can fix positive learning experiences deep down in the unconscious. Every time we recognize the smell, the learning experience is also activated.

Exercise: To Give Up Smoking

Therapeutic trances aimed at stopping cigarette smoking work by:

✧ uncovering what smoking means for the individual smoker,

✧ replacing smoking with other rituals that are less damaging to the person's health, and

✧ fixing the positive learning experience of not having to smoke in the unconscious through new olfactory experiences.

Smokers often smoke in order to:

✧ set a smoke signal, claiming a territory by smell;

✧ take up more room, find inner greatness, expand;

✧ gain more air, distance, and freedom;

✧ watch the smoke and thus express themselves;

✧ have something to hold in their hand when they are in company;

✧ be united with others by a shared cloud of smoke; or

✧ envelop themselves in smoke—for example, to intoxicate themselves.

There are no limits to the imagination in producing new rituals for old needs or in examining old needs and perhaps finding new solutions.

Trance Induction Through Tasting

The sense of taste is assigned to the second chakra. On the one hand, this sense has to do with a physical sensation and our own experience of pleasure or repugnance, and, on the other hand, with the way we experience life with others, in the family, in a group, in society, and so forth.

Taste is related to fine-tuning on the noncognitive level. Long before the brain can explain why something is revolting, "leaves a nasty taste in the mouth," or "goes down well," the stomach knows it already, because it has a feeling for what is good for us and what isn't. To feel in your stomach means to orient yourself by your taste.

It can be assumed that the many herbs, mineral substances, and kinds of meat that humans have consumed over the course of civilization have demanded various sacrifices in order for us to be able to distinguish between poisonous and nonpoisonous, tasty and unpalatable, healing and harmful, because taste has as much to do with experience as with digesting and utilizing. What is agreeable and what isn't? There are also many differences from one person to the next: As the old saying goes, one man's meat is another man's poison. Of course, there are some poisons that don't agree with anybody. Nevertheless, when some so-called poisons are taken in small portions, they can be effective remedies.

It's amazing how much experience has taken place, and still needs to occur, to test for incompatibilities. Today, we use animals for such tests. In the past, however, it was likely that people tested themselves to see what agreed with them and what didn't, or tested the substance on lower-ranking people. Thus the emperor's food taster was constantly in danger of being poisoned. Today, poison is still a prevalent method for murder.

Poisoning occurs again and again, even if it is not done deliberately by someone. It results from polluted drinking water, spoilt food, sick animals, or vegetables or fruit that have been subjected to radiation. Poisoning can also be caused by the manipulation of food or by certain environmental influences. Ailments, illness, or even death can be brought on by something we ate or drank.

Therefore, food is not just a matter of taste but also of trust. At the beginning of its life, a child is completely dependent on its mother's milk, and, later, on what it gets to eat and drink from its mother or nurse. Moving the food around in its mouth as children do (and not only children), spitting out porridge, or the strong refusal of certain other foods, may be annoying to the adult in charge, yet an important childhood step on the way to developing individual taste.

What we put in our mouths should be good for us. It should nourish, develop, strengthen, cleanse, or heal us. How can we know whether we can trust a certain food and swallow it, or whether it would be better to spit it out?

Here, it is helpful to listen to your intuition and appeal to your senses, without switching off your logical mind, of course. When tasting a certain food, you should not be led solely by your senses, emotions, and desires. In the past, tasting during trance has supplied me with important answers regarding what is actually good for me and what isn't. Furthermore, specific autosuggestions, when applied consciously, can help alleviate eating disorders as well as drinking problems.

Many metaphors commonly used in speech allude to eating and tasting being connected to absorbing and loving, or their opposites, ejecting and detesting. As you read the following sentences and phrases, pay attention to what associations they bring up for you.

You are good enough to eat! What you say is not to my taste. Wow, she's got great taste! I don't want much, just a little taste. I have acquired a taste for this. He gobbled her up (or devoured her) with his eyes. That makes my mouth water. He buttered her up. That goes down like honey. He ate his heart out for something. Something is hard to chew, and hard to get down. Chew on that for a while. That is hard to digest. Ooh, that left a nasty taste in my mouth! This really makes me sick. I can't stomach it. A bitter pill to swallow. To bite the bullet. The sweetness of life. He looked sour. To be drunk with joy. A delicious feeling.

There's also this proverb: "The way to a man's heart is through his stomach."

Exercise: Trance Induction—Making the Mouth Water

Here, you can test your own autosuggestive skills. Are you able to put yourself into such a state of anticipation that it makes your mouth water? Can you stimulate the flow of saliva with your imagination? And, if so, what exactly do you have to do to achieve this?

Some Important Tips and Preliminary Exercises

It's helpful to relax the jaw, and thus go into a state where you don't have to suppress anything. All the grim determination that may have made you clench your teeth all the time up to this point and made you fight your way through life now gives way to a feeling of sheer pleasure. It helps to part the lips a little, or maybe even open the mouth a bit wider, and to close the eyes and concentrate on the pleasant effect of water. You could also reflect on how the process of liquefaction makes life easier and brings you closer to solutions. Keep a hold on the feeling of desire for a while that is developing inside of you slowly but surely, so that you can really feel the saliva collecting in your mouth before you swallow it as usual. Let the pleasure spread a little more than you normally do.

Of course, it also helps to imagine consuming certain foods and drinks, considering that *what* we eat and drink is not the only important thing, but also *how* we do it. In your imagination, concentrate on the first little sip, the very first bite, a trial sip, a tidbit, nothing more. Let the taste permeate and melt in your mouth. Enjoy it. Don't look upon eating and drinking as a matter of survival, but instead consider the nuances of taste and flavor as if you were a discriminating gourmet, for whom only the best is good enough.

Now proceed in your imagination, letting yourself swallow the delicious tidbit. How is the aftertaste? Allow yourself to be very critical, evaluating the aftertaste as if it was the taste itself.

Now let a little time pass in your imagination-say, about 30 minutes. At this point, you have eaten what you only tasted earlier and it has arrived in your stomach. What do you feel like now?

Let more time pass in your imagination, about two hours. How do you feel now, once what you ate is digested in your stomach? How do you think you will sleep the coming night with this food in your body? Set yourself the highest standards—after all, it's your body!

Often our eyes are bigger than our stomachs. Something may look good but still not agree with us. You may think something looks irresistible, and find that the first bite bears this out. But as soon as you take a second or a third bite, you realize that the food doesn't agree with you after all. And frequently we are only aware of how disagreeable a food is after we have already stuffed ourselves with it. Sometimes the stomach feels knocked out, and so do we. Prevent this mishap by developing your skills of taste, so that your intuition will tell you in advance what won't agree with you later on!

Exercise: Shamanic Taste Test

Imagine that you are a shaman and are trying to contact the food spirit. Then imagine that there is a spirit living in every plant. Now go on to imagine that this spirit wants to tell you something while you put the plant in which it lives on your tongue. You are seated comfortably and are relaxed. Now, as with all shamanic journeys, the drumming and the rattling starts and leads you into trance. You don't have to swallow anything, and can spit out what you taste at any time.

Instead, as you put the sample on your tongue, you may be "kidnapped" or "seized" and find yourself in a fantasy world, as in other trance journeys. Here, the food spirit may simply emerge from the dark or be discerned as a shadow in the background. Sometimes the spirits only make themselves known through a vague feeling in the stomach.

On the level of the logical human mind, you may look askance at meeting the spirits of plants. But it is useful to come into contact with them, because they sharpen our sense of taste and our sampling, helping us determine whether a particular food is good for us or not. Consider subjecting every type of food that you eat first to a shamanic test of this kind.

Exercise: Imagining Eating Certain Foods

Listen to your body, in order to give it what it needs.

Frequently people who are ill have an aversion toward those foods that are bad for them; for example, people with a liver disorder feel sick merely thinking about fried food. Develop the discernment of which foods are good for you and which aren't by using your imagination. First picture everything that you want to eat. Create a vision of what you are about to consume. Then imagine eating these foods while being alert to your body's needs, preferences, and dislikes. It's amazing how often your body will tell you exactly what it needs if you just listen attentively without being influenced by preconceived ideas. Your body will also tell you how much and how fast you should eat.

Help for Eating Disorders

A variety of expressions connoting eating—like "demolish," "bolt down," and "put away"—shows that the body sometimes functions as a waste chute. "You'll eat what you're given" is a rule that ignores the needs of the body. Eating in reserve is another way to overload the body and misuse it as a storage tank. A counter-reaction can be anorexia, a pathological fear of weight gain that can lead to faulty eating patterns, malnutrition, and excessive weight loss. Although in our culture being thin-up to a point—is socially acceptable and even desirable, this is a despicable way of treating the body. With anorexia, ideals of immaculateness and purity are often predominant, and there is the wish to protect the body from the insult of stuffing it with "garbage."

Anorexia mainly affects young women, as does another eating disorder: bulimia. Women with bulimia alternate between gulping food down and vomiting it up, thereby completely overtaxing and "insulting" the organism. Furthermore, feelings of guilt and shame as well as unconscious strategies having to do with self-punishment do not put an end to this eating disorder, but rather support a mode of behavior that is completely out of balance.

Means of trance induction involving taste can help those with eating disorders by confirming the value of a person's own taste and anchoring this in one's eating habits. The appreciation of a person's own taste leads away from contempt for the body and the senses and toward an attentiveness that builds up and maintains self-esteem. In addition, eating slowly and consciously prevents unconscious mechanisms from operating automatically. Eating this way can even turn into a form of meditation.

Support for Giving Up Bad Habits

After a period of fasting, it is very important to resume your normal eating habits slowly. At the beginning, everything tastes especially delicious. But then the stimuli of taste decreases and the old, careless eating habits take over again, diminishing the value and the effect of the fast to a large extent. Likewise, diets, during which the body had regenerated wonderfully, are often ruined by falling back into former, bad eating habits, which now return even more strongly.

Here, trance induction can help by addressing the relapse and imagining it so clearly that it is felt physically. The advantage of having a healthy body becomes so obvious that we begin to develop a taste for everything that will promote health.

With alcohol, sugar, or nicotine addictions, taste meditations can lead to abandoning these well-loved, yet destructive habits. The loss of not fulfilling such forbidden desires is offset by the benefit of finding pleasure in tasting food that does your body good.

You can give up negative habits through will, reason, and rigid discipline, and persuade yourself with tricks of autosuggestion, but you can also switch over to a new taste that in its sensory nature is just as good as the old one. Often, however, it is not so much the body and its sensory needs that hinder a change as a spirit of defiance. You've probably heard people say, "I'd rather die than give up smoking. What else do I get out of life?" But once defiance has given way to curiosity, it is quite possible that a new taste for life will develop during trance.

Trance Induction Through Seeing

Seeing is assigned to the third chakra, and is traditionally connected to passion. Seeing makes it possible to take something in by a look, which can have a consuming or devouring character. The element of fire is also assigned to the third chakra, and the eyes can betray the condition of a person's inner fire. Is it out of control so that it governs the person, or has it died, producing a lifeless, cold, or cloudy look? A warm look shows that a person takes care of and nourishes his or her inner fire, and has transformed the explosive volcano of impulses and desires into warmth and light.

The word "see" literally means "to follow with the eyes" and is related to the Latin word *sequi,* to follow, as in the word "consequence." Seeing also has the meaning of recognizing, or noticing. The following phrases, strangely enough, have to do with the invisible or describe mental processes that, unnoticed from the outside, take place inside of us: to see in, to see through, to see about, to see to, "I don't see why," "I'll have to see." Therefore, "to look" is also a directed perception.

There are four dimensions of seeing: color, form, physical depth, and movement. Sight is the sensory channel that can take up and store the greatest amount of impressions in the shortest time. The most important means of communication in the brain is pictures, because they gather and structure information in larger units, helping us to get an idea of the world around us. We could describe the smallest unit of consciousness with a term taken from computer language: a bit. Thus, the present, contrary to general belief, is capable of extension, as it represents a bit in the subjective experience of a person. Only when this bit has fallen into place can the present be recognized as such.

71

Seeing images is an extraordinarily fast process. Seeing is not better than hearing and feeling, but the consciousness is able to concentrate on it faster, and it also appeals to the unconscious. That's why it is the most economical method of storing a lot of information at once. Moreover, the processing of information is done by means of visual images. The speed at which the brain constantly processes new information is so incredibly fast that thoughts and feelings lag behind like thunder after lightning. We always create an image, or imagine something, before we switch on the other senses. Only reflex actions have the same speed, which is why shock is sometimes the only possible way to switch off our inner pictures, because it tricks the brain and puts it on autopilot.

Vision plays a major role in the conscious, well-considered processing of a plan, so it's not without reason that we use the word "vision" to denote a picture of the future. It is neither a feeling nor a thought but just a picture. Seeing is the preferred sensory channel of modern times. Visual types find it much easier to get along in this age of style and design than contemplative, reflective philosophers. This trend started long before television came into our lives, at the beginning of modern times, in the Renaissance period. At that time, perspective was discovered, and its use in art radically changed the way people felt about life. The world was moved to a distance and placed in proportion, giving human beings a new sense of control over their environment. Optical instruments were discovered and brought faraway objects closer, whereas what was close at hand and familiar became strange when viewed through a microscope. The world gained new dimensions—at first, only on the visual plane.

The word "dimension" itself has to do with measuring, which in turn depends on phenomena existing physically side by side. Measuring represents an important level of development of human evolution, individually as well as collectively. Sight is a prerequisite for comparison, and with distinguishing, comparing, and evaluating, envy came into world. In many myths and fairy tales possessiveness plays an important role. The evil look is a look of covetousness, which can be banned with the amulet of the magic eye. People feared not only the envy of their neighbors but also the envy of the gods. It is said that the look itself has an influence, as it represents more than just a passive absorption of the surroundings. The well-known head-in-the-sand approach is based on the incorrect assumption that seeing nothing means not taking part in what is happening or having any responsibility for it. If the sense of sight is clouded or otherwise obscured, we believe that we are removed from the impressions of the present. This is a fatal error of judgment, which occurs even among many educated people—take, for example, the spectators of the first atomic explosions, who only donned spectacles to protect themselves from the radiation.

No sensory channel is as strongly subjected to selection through subjective filters of experience as seeing, so it's not without reason that we talk about rose-tinted glasses and the like. And every idea or illusion, regardless of which sensory channel it is associated with, is related to the making of images. Delusion (being blind to something) is also a visual phenomenon, even if it has a much wider metaphoric meaning. Some religions do not allow an image of God to be made. A picture fixes something in the imagination and interrupts the organic or cosmic flow of change. But omnipresence is attributed to God, as symbolized by the all-seeing eye of God.

Linguistic Metaphors

Regard every metaphor that follows as a verbal image, and translate it into a symbol—in other words, try to picture in your mind what the metaphor is saying. Pay attention to whether or not you find it easy to call up pictures in your mind, and whether or not words have a vivid effect on you.

✧ Love at first sight

✧ To see something through to the end

✧ To see through something, such as a deception

✧ To get an overview

✧ To look after someone

✧ To look back over something

✧ To look up to someone you admire

✧ To look down upon someone

✧ To look down one's nose at someone

✧ To look forward to something

✧ To look into a matter

✧ To keep an eye out for something

✧ To keep one's eyes open

✧ To look to the future, or the past

✧ To look with disdain, contempt, etc.

✧ To look askance

✧ To look the other way

✧ To turn a blind eye

✧ To look with both eyes open

✧ To grant an inside view

✧ To look at it from this angle

✧ To see something one way or another

✧ To see eye to eye

✧ In my view

✧ The way I see it

✧ Something is clear/unclear

✧ A hazy view

✧ To see why

✧ To look at things in another light

✧ To appear in an unfavorable light

✧ To be in the limelight

✧ To stand by and watch something happen

✧ Not to see the point of something

✧ To see red

✧ To be in a black mood

✧ In view of this

✧ A point of view

✧ To see the world in black and white

✧ To see with rose-colored glasses

✧ To wear blinders

✧ To be blind when it comes to something

✧ To close your eyes on something

✧ Something is overshadowed by something else

✧ To have a clouded view

✧ To have a biased view

✧ To draw a veil over something

✧ To throw dust in somebody's eyes

✧ Not to trust my eyes

✧ To see it with my own eyes

✧ The dark side of his personality

✧ An ugly matter

✧ A transparent argument

✧ An obscure point

✧ A brilliant author who has unveiled something

✧ A bright mind and a precise observer who holds up a mirror to society

✧ To show the unpainted truth

✧ To have a wide horizon

✧ To have a new perspective

✧ To draw a clear line

✧ To be the focus of attention

✧ You can't pull the wool over his eyes

✧ I'm not blind—that's how it looks to me

✧ To picture something

✧ To create a favorable picture

✧ That doesn't fit the picture

✧ That puts color into the picture

✧ That colored his view

✧ He revealed his true colors

Proverbs

"Appearances can be deceptive."
"All that glitters is not gold."

Exercise: "Swallowing the Eyes"

This trance induction is recommended if you want to undertake a journey into the body. This can be journey into your own body or the body of a partner. When practicing with a partner, lie down next to each other, slightly touching with your hands or fingers. Agree beforehand who is going to play the active part, the traveler. Then a drumming or rattling will begin, which is most suitable for this form of archaic trance induction. Limit the exercise to 15 minutes. Simply imagine yourself swallowing your own eyes, and then let them wander about inside your body. Often the eyes develop their own dynamics as soon as they have reached the gullet, as if they knew the way of their own accord. Mostly, you travel with the flow of the blood or take your bearings from other moving bodily fluids.

The trance journey comes to an end when the drumming or rattling stops. Don't worry—your eyes will be back in the right place then, so that you can open them and look at the outside world.

Exercise: Turning the Eyes Upward and Back—Making a Backward Somersault into the Cosmos

Close your eyes, and look up as far as you can behind your closed lids, as if you wanted to touch the top of your skull from the inside, and then look even further backward. This feels like tumbling over or making a backward somersault, and it catapults you into cosmic space, which you can imagine as an infinite black room. Here, invisibly, all information is stored, which you can now call up in trance. Instead, you can let yourself float into a blue room, which radiates endless breadth, clearness, and peace. Or you can transport yourself into a green room, for relaxation and regeneration.

Limit this exercise to a few breaths, or to not more than three minutes. You will be surprised to find how little time you will need to cover an infinite distance outside of all imaginable dimensions! Define your goal before undertaking this exercise: either to let yourself be inspired and receive unusual, new thoughts (black), to improve your powers of concentration (blue), or to put yourself in a state of repose (green). Green is also the most agreeable color for the eyes, and it is suitable for taking a break from work, especially if you work with a computer. Yellow lightens your mood, white neutralizes, and red activates.

Entering Trance Through Colors

Corresponding to the four categories of seeing—color, form, depth, and movement—there are four groups of visual trance induction. Naturally, combinations are not only possible but also desirable, because they deepen the experience and supply a greater variety and stimulation.

Colors affect our psychological condition and have a clearly perceptible influence on our moods. Their influence even goes so far as to alter our physical condition, and can be measured as an increase or decrease of blood pressure or as a pattern of brain waves. Colors not only affect people but also other living beings, even plants. This has been tested and documented.

When you start to experiment with trance colors, it is important to approach the new experience without prejudice and to first try it out thoroughly before you read interpretations and traditional classifications. Preferences and dislikes certainly say a great deal about you, but they can also change very quickly according to your needs and your present situation. It is best not to start at the minus pole but at the maximum level of desire. What color is the most agreeable to you, strengthens you, supports you, stimulates you, calms you, or reminds you of something pleasant at this very moment? Cut some strips of material, each in a different color, and every now and then place them in front of you to test which color suits you best that day. Colors radiate, and not only in a symbolic way. Stand on such a piece of material, and you will feel how the color transmits its vibrations to you.

In my training courses, I set up a trance game in which the participants crept into single-colored cloth sacks and stayed there during the drumming or rattling trance induction, thus experiencing the vibrations of the color in a color trance. There were, for example, a black sack (alluding to the endless cosmos), a red "plasma" sack (in connection with symbolic or real birth processes), and a blue sack for vision. There also was a cloth tunnel 15 meters (about 50 feet) long in the colors of the rainbow, starting with dark red and ending with violet. The color range corresponded to the colors of the chakras, or energy centers, and creeping through them was comparable to a journey through the body along the vertical energy line, starting either at the head (violet) or at the feet (dark red).

Every traveler had set him- or herself a different task, or trance destination. Some wanted to undergo the process from the top to the bottom, and thereby experience something that in esoteric traditions is described as the process of incarnation. They got into contact with their imagination, desires, hopes, and fears related to this. But most of the participants wanted to proceed from the bottom to the top—that is, to reach for higher things. They wanted to increase their vibrations. The higher up in the body the chakras are, the faster they vibrate. At the uppermost point, the vibrations are so fast and high pitched, they are almost unbearable. Often this is experienced as a state of ecstasy. Sometimes it is sufficient to imagine fast and high-pitched vibrations in violet, in order to experience a euphoric condition of spaciousness and "lifting off."

Those who work a great deal with colors use them more as signals and are no longer dependent on the actual physical experience—for example, you see red and think red. The physical experience is triggered by the signal. There are traditional, ceremonial assignments of colors to gods, psychological conditions, and physical reactions, which can be found reflected in the colors of ritual clothing (such as priests' vestments). In the trance cult of the Gnaua tribe in Morocco, colors play an important role. For instance, over the course of a trance night, various gods or aspects of one god appear through colors. But they don't merely appear as a phenomenon of the outside world, but are also experienced by the dancers as a reality of the inner world. Outside and inside correspond to each other, the group is attuned to certain vibrations through the cult, and this shows itself in a color. Then the body of the lead dancer is wrapped in a large piece of cloth of that color. Veil dances originally had a ritual meaning too.

Colored light as a specific trance induction can be combined with other trance techniques-for example, with a massage or trance dance. The kinesthetic sensation that you experience is supported by the vibrations of the color. You dance differently to red than to blue, in a blinding flood of light through the dark. Colored light also plays a role in certain techniques of alternative medicine.

The classic Mesmer lamp has four panes of glass in four different colors. As the lamp revolves, the focus of attention jumps from one color to the next, producing a colorful blend of visual impulses in the consciousness. You can also give a different tint to normal reality simply by wearing tinted glasses.

In the wonderful Islamic mosques, great importance is attributed to the colorful play of light shining through the stained-glass windows. It symbolizes the manifold divine aspects of God. In the Jewish esoteric doctrine, the cabala, the single divinity is broken down into many different aspects as soon as it becomes visible—this is similar to white light refracted in a spectrum.

Entering Trance Through Shapes

A point can even be considered a shape. Staring at one point is a trance technique that is probably familiar to many of you. Often and involuntarily during everyday life, our eyes are caught and stare at one point. The concomitant facial expression is empty and shows an inner absence. If we decide voluntarily not to let our eyes roam or be caught by one interesting object after another, we will experience a concentration that will even increase with repeated practice.

Staring at one point, which can also be replaced by fixing our eyes on an object—a candle flame, a flower in a vase, a crack in the wall—gives direction to our attention, focusing it as through a lens. However, our unconscious becomes more and more active, the more our conscious attention is focused and calmed down in its volatility. Then unconscious events and processes, which we could describe as inventions of our fantasy, but which also represent a reality that is always present below the threshold of our consciousness, start to unwind and reveal themselves on the surface. If we close our eyes after such incessant staring, then such events will take place behind our closed eyelids as if on a stage or a screen, and they will seem to have taken on a life of their own.

Staring at a point, a line, or any nongeometrical shape is a tried-and-tested method for dealing with pain through trance. This is not just any kind of distraction, but a very specific intervention that draws the attention to itself so strongly that our perception has no room for anything except the shape of the envisaged object. Even the content is not so important. The only important thing is the shape, which seems to fill our consciousness. The form of a flower or a petal can gain a completely new meaning in this way. Whereas color trances deal with emotional content, shape trances give you an idea of what the mind can expect when it has freed itself from the straitjacket of identifying with content. Formal aesthetics only shows itself when the eyes are fixed on the pattern and no longer cling to the usual meanings and personal evaluations.

This refraining from individual identification causes a condition of distance and dissociation. Sometimes, during unbearable pain or other overwhelming feelings, this happens by itself more or less as an autonomous regulation of the organism, which in this way protects itself from an excess of stimuli. Possibly it is from these involuntary experiences that the consciously controlled trance techniques of concentrating on shape developed.

Visualization is another trance technique, representing an internalization of external visual stimuli from the outside, which are called up before the mind's eye. Colors are frequently visualized in trance journeys to stimulate, calm down, or activate inner forces, especially the body's defense and healing mechanisms. Visualizing shapes, however, helps in concept development and project building. Geometric forms can reflect inner thoughts so that other people can also get an idea of the concept or envisage a project vividly. In trance techniques dealing mainly with mental tasks, we are confronted correspondingly with abstract shapes relating not so much to the content as to the form.

Sketches are not realistic pictures but symbolic representations of developed thoughts in graphic form. Someone who is visually gifted and has direct access to shapes finds it easier to express the structures of his or her thoughts than someone less visually attuned. The imagination works with such formal images, which are mentally conceived (received) and materially projected (designed). In creativity training, such formal visual approaches are indispensable.

A very useful trance technique is to imagine time as a line (see the book *Time Lines* by Robert Dilts). If you want to envisage how to get from A to B, from desire to fulfillment, from a project concept to the realization of the project, from setting the task to reaching the goal, it can be helpful to draw a time line. Or you can spread it out on the floor. Then time becomes a path on which you can walk. But before you walk along this path, see it in front of you with your mind's eye.

The path can take various forms: It can be a straight or a wavy line. You have to be able to envision these forms in order to judge the quality of the path. When turning this into a kinesthetic experience by actually drawing it on the floor and walking along it, you might get additional information, but at the beginning there is just the picture. The picture has magic powers, because it defines the reality of a future experience. You don't merely envision something; you form reality after your own vision.

In the esoteric traditions of Asia, certain shapes are known to have a magical effect on reality if you look at them. Take, for example, the circular form of the mandala, which gathers and orders reality in a large circle. The drawing of a mandala brings about order and insight. It also has this effect on a person who looks at it. The psychologist C. G. Jung discovered the importance of mandalas for the psyche of modern people in the Western world, and classified it as a basic need. Even, or perhaps especially, mentally disturbed people tend to want to see the world within the form of a mandala.

Higher demands on abstraction are made by yantras, which are geometrical diagrams in which mostly triangular forms fit into one another. The triangle has a strong dynamic effect, forming certain proportions and relations that are fleeting and transitory and appear to be upside down and in danger of toppling over. Ideally, all harmonic relations should correspond to the proportions of an isosceles triangle, but often one side is unexpectedly drawn out and the sensitive harmony is immediately lost. Trance techniques that work with the visualization of triangles are for advanced practitioners, for they understand the delicate balance among three factors, between which a stable relationship can only be established with difficulty and for a short time.

Visualizing a rectangle, especially a square, strengthens the inner condition of stability and integration. In some exercises, the system of coordinates, or intersecting axes connecting the four sides of the rectangle, is used to create a clear picture of the connection between two opposing sides of something. The cross formed by the vertical and the horizontal axes is an ancient symbol of orientation, and has served as a practical navigation tool in the form of a compass card since time immemorial. In processes of mediation between opposites and of centering and concentrating, the intersection point of the axes has the additional meaning of a center point from which such processes are more easily executed.

Entering Trance Using the Three-Dimensionality of the Visual Experience of Space

Here, we come to the topic of the perception of background and foreground, which plays a leading role in Gestalt psychology, which is concerned with the individual's response to configurational wholes. The plasticity and the depth of experience as well as the perception of distance, proportions, and physical dimensions depend on the ability to judge distance by sight alone. To do this, we first have to perceive the object in the foreground, which seems to merge into the background, as a separate shape. Our ability to separate the object from the background, however, is dependent on our habits of perception, a quality that is used in working jigsaw puzzles. These confusing puzzles, which make us aware of the prejudices of our immediate perceptions, can be seen as a metaphor and can tell us something about life. We can put ourselves at will into a condition in which the whole world appears like a picture puzzle, and in which we can never be sure what shapes will emerge on any given day.

This exercise, which is among the more demanding trance techniques, brings about an openness in us that starts with perception and leads to a way of thinking far exceeding a superficial causal and linear logic. This is why multidimensional picture puzzles are so popular with pioneers of a new way of thinking ("thinking the unthinkable"). Not without reason is there a homophony of the words "eye" and "I." The aim is to let the eye become more flexible, so that it can adjust its perceptions faster and give up its habitually fixed way of looking at things.

Trance techniques that work with visualizing beams of light belong here too. Of course, there is also light focused on one point or diffused light, but most of the time the spotlight, as we know it from the theater, is used to move something from the background (the unconscious, the past, the self-evident, the usual) into the foreground and into the focus of our conscious attention, bidding us to take a closer look at it by highlighting it.

Visualizing an inner picture enlarged or reduced in size, glossy or matte, color or black-and-white, sharp or blurred (or taken with a soft-focus lens, as NLP trance therapy calls it)—all this involves dealing with visual trances and requires a certain talent and a visual inclination.

I remember one time beginning a trance induction for a Protestant congregation with the words, "And now we turn our eyes to the inside and look into ourselves." I noticed the uncertainty in the room. Their eyes, far from being closed, were watching me suspiciously; the entire congregation was one big question mark.

Entering Trance Through Visually Perceived Movement

Most means of visual trance induction fall into this category. Visual impulses in the form of constant stimuli have achieved great effects when the aim was to influence brain-wave patterns and thus a person's inner state with minimal effort. Did you happen to see the Disney movie of Kipling's *Jungle Book?* Kaa, the snake, tries to put a magic spell on Mowgli, the rabbit, with rotating spiral movements in his eyes. Mowgli seems to have become completely hypnotized, with spirals showing up in his eyes too, when Baghira, the panther, arrives just in time and breaks the spell. The circling spirals are patterns in movement that are especially potent in inducing trance.

The so-called brain machines (or mind machines) work along similar lines, transferring visual impulses onto the closed eyelids through glasses. Behind the lids appear dancing patterns of great beauty. These patterns, however, are not only entertaining but also influence the inner condition of a person. Different patterns and rhythms have different effects. The buttons on the control panel show a whole menu of possible programs, ranging from deep relaxation (for overcoming sleeping disorders) to the stimulation of relaxed, but conscious thinking (as needed for rethinking in crisis situations or for thinking up new solutions to a problem). Obviously, the brain "learns" by imitating—it lets the new patterns take effect as the result of rhythmically emitted visual stimuli and adapts to them.

This phenomenon has also produced a tragic effect at least once. On a particular avenue in France, inexplicable car accidents often occurred in midday when the sun was shining or in the early evening when the sun's rays were low and slanted. The road was straight, and there was no obstacle in the drivers' way. There was a speed limit, and speeding was not found to be the reason for the accidents. The surviving drivers all spoke about a tiredness that had suddenly come upon them, as if there was some kind of jinx to the area. The "clouding over of consciousness" mentioned by the survivors supplied the explanation: The play of light and shadow from the sun had an influence on the activity of their brain waves.

Flickering light, as can be observed in a fire in a hearth at night and as created by candles in a church, has probably always been used for trance induction. A shimmering, gleaming, or glittering surface, like that of a lake reflecting the sun, or the highly polished surface of a shiny object, such as the traditional crystal ball used by fortune-tellers, invites the eyes to rest on it and to dissolve the consciously fixed focus, causing a slight squint; if this is induced deliberately, we speak of the techniques of bi-focusing and de-focusing. Movement only has a minimal part to play here, but it still operates, because the focus jumps and eventually splits (bi-focusing, as in double vision) or is enlarged (de-focusing, or the dissolving of visual acuity).

In films, optical means are applied to achieve a mood of unreality. I will never forget the sunlight flashing through the leaves of the trees in *Rashomon*.

If you want to experiment with this kind of trance induction, you don't have to rush out to the nearest disco with strobe lights or buy yourself a mind machine. It is sufficient to look into a strong light source, perhaps the sun, while you cross your hands in front of your face with your fingers spread far apart so that the light can only penetrate in certain places. Then move your hands back and forth so that the places move and you get the impression of flickering light.

Exercise: Softening the Vision and Letting Go

Perhaps you remember having to drive in the darkness during a heavy snowstorm and how difficult it was to see the road through the dancing snowflakes? Do you recall how hard it was to distinguish things through the windshield and how tempting it was to simply stop driving and let yourself be swallowed up by the indistinguishable? This trance exercise deals with the "soft look," which doesn't perceive anything clearly but instead dissolves the world in a shimmer. All fixations, all rigid borders and contours, all familiar shapes disappear in a fog or a mist, and you see the world as a play of colors, a complex pattern, or as something fleeting or constantly changing.

Exercise: Seeing the World with New Eyes

With a melted, soft look, you can see the world in a new way. During such moments of pleasant tiredness (not when you are driving!), we often gain important insights. Relaxing and relieving the eyes, which no longer have to look greedily or compulsively, has an effect on our psychological condition. Imagine that you have multiple eyes, like insects do, and a radius of vision of 180 degrees so that you can take in everything at the borders of your field of vision. Enlarge this already very wide radius of vision even further by imagining that you have eyes at the back of your neck. These eyes open up like the golden eyes of a very wise and very old toad in a fairy tale, and they see everything that happens in the background, in the depth of your unconscious, and also in the expanses of the consciousness of everyone around you. Suddenly you can see through the obvious, and you find your view extending to the bottom of the lake.

Do this exercise when you want to relax and assume a playful make-believe attitude. Pretend that you are in a fairy tale, so that you can experience fabulous things again like in your childhood. Or image that you are dreaming. Grant yourself the luxury of experiencing dreamlike things in the midst of everyday life, even though you are not dreaming. You will be surprised by how grateful your eyes will be and how willingly they will perform their everyday duty of well-focused differentiation.

Trance Induction Through Touch

The sense of touch involves much more than mere touching. It conveys the sensory experience of feeling, on the physical as well as the figurative level. Everything that can be felt has something to do with touch. Touch is only possible through the skin, which is our largest organ. The skin has two functions: It forms the boundary of the body, giving us firm physical contours, and thereby "roping us off" and protecting us from everything else around us. But it is also a receptive organ: Our skin connects us to the outside world. We breathe through the skin, just as we discharge waste products and toxic substances through it.

By means of touching and being touched, we acquire our initial knowledge of the world. This is first a kinesthetic experience of the body, and only over the course of increasing abstraction does it find its expression in speech.

Feeling as a physical, sensory experience is brought into connection with emotions rather than with thought, because it is more closely related to them. Thought is, you might say, at the other end of the "information processing line." Feeling can be very sensuous and direct, but with some people it is immediately translated into emotional categories. In this case, they are not responding to physical stimuli, but are calling up past interpretations of them. This results in equations—for example, a stomachache could equal fear, defensiveness, dislike, or illness, although it could be related to something very definite, like having eaten a greasy sausage!

The sense of touch, which in the kinesthetic sense includes movement as well, is a necessary prerequisite for experience of any kind. Many words for states of consciousness relate to a physical experience: to touch and be touched, to be moved, to get into touch, to have a feeling, to sense, sensitivity, instinctive feeling, empathy (from Greek *pathos*, feelings), tact (from the Latin verb *tangere*, to touch), contact (literally, to come together by touching), conflict (to come together by beating), and confusion (to come together by flowing into each other).

Interestingly, the sense of touch is assigned to the fourth chakra, the heart chakra.

It is the "heart" of the senses, the place where all the other senses flow together and are gathered in a single experience. I can picture something, or have an impression of it, and I don't just hear what a person says to me, but it also touches me. No other sense makes me take such a critical look at my surroundings.

Here, experiences are like translations: Something approaches me, and only through my own experience do I find a parallel that responds to the outside stimulus with an inner movement. It is said that a person is connected to everything with his or her heart. Of course, it's not the heart as an organ that is meant here, but the level of consciousness that mediates between the "heart" (which is equated with the seat of our feelings) and the mind. It is the level of contact and communication. I can open or close my heart, meaning that I can let it become wide and expansive or experience it as small, narrow, or hardened.

It is not surprising that the traditional methods of trance induction, as we know of them from the study of religions, are actually all of a kinesthetic nature. The alteration of consciousness is reached through a change in the body and the body's (physical) feeling. Mostly, the phase of extended consciousness—which is reflected in states of enthusiasm, emotion, obsession, enlightenment, and vision, and which is the true aim of trance—is preceded by a phase of kinesthetic trance induction, during which the consciousness is blurred, disturbed, or completely switched off.

In some possession cults, the trance dancer recovers his normal consciousness after being possessed but cannot remember the phase of being possessed. In fact, it is not even expected of him, although those present witness a god or a spirit moving into the body of the dancer and being revealed in the dance. To have a memory of this could be an unnecessary strain on the trance dancer. So, here the consciousness is only present in its collective form of the attending congregation.

Thus, kinesthetic trances are not necessarily connected to a transformation or an expansion of consciousness, which may be one reason why in Western traditions they moved more and more into the background until they were viewed disparagingly or finally forgotten. Only children are allowed to spin around in circles, wildly flailing their arms. However, adults do grant themselves a turn on the roller coaster, whereby they experience the thrill of speed, of imbalance, of losing a sense of the ground under their feet, and of seeing the world upside down.

Kinesthetic trances bring immediate, sensuous pleasure—for most people. Others feel sick or experience them as an effort that makes them perspire. Kinesthetic trances always affect the entire body and appeal to the senses. This experience makes demands on the whole person. Kinesthetic trances often last longer than visual or auditory ones, and it is more difficult to distance yourself from what you have experienced, because it "goes under the skin." More than other trances, kinesthetic trances call for trust or a certain willingness to take risks. It is difficult to break off in the middle of the process, and here the trance, as a process, develops its own dynamics more than in other types of trance.

If you are not quite sure how far you want to go and would like to get acquainted with the feeling of your own body, it is recommended to translate metaphors in speech into physical expressions as a preliminary exercise. Use the metaphors below as models for charades, which you could play with other people during a workshop.

Linguistic Metaphors

✧ It gets under my skin

✧ It makes my skin crawl

✧ This gives me a push

✧ To run with the pack

✧ To run amok

✧ A kick in the pants

✧ My blood froze

✧ Somebody walked over my grave

✧ I shudder to think

✧ It's weighing heavily on my mind

✧ Weighed down with sorrow

✧ My knees are shaking

✧ That got me down

✧ The heart jumps with delight

✧ I'm seething with rage

✧ Put somebody back on his feet again

✧ Put one's foot down

✧ I feel washed out

✧ To have one's feet on the ground

✧ To keep in step

✧ To take steps

✧ It turned my stomach

✧ He took to his heels

✧ I had a lump in my throat

✧ He felt left out

✧ To push someone into the background

✧ To feel uneasy

✧ I wouldn't like to be in his shoes

✧ I wish the ground would swallow me up

✧ To get to grips with something

✧ To tread carefully

✧ Something is going wrong

✧ To get off the track

✧ To get the upper hand

✧ You can't really get the hang of him

✧ He stays aloof

✧ I don't get it

✧ She was floating on air

✧ He dragged himself along

✧ He came to life again

✧ Heave a sigh of relief

✧ This moves me to tears

✧ I would handle it this way

✧ He is slow on the uptake

✧ He's dense

✧ You always have to put your foot in it

✧ I feel rotten

✧ A cool guy

✧ You've missed the boat

✧ I felt a great emptiness

✧ His heart was in his mouth

✧ She was hard-hearted, warm-hearted

✧ That's a load off my mind

✧ Completely lulled

✧ You're pulling my leg

✧ You are getting on my nerves

✧ That leaves me cold

✧ A hot dance

✧ This is a kick

✧ This really turns me on

✧ This drives me mad

✧ Let's go back to the beginning

✧ I'm getting out of doing it

Exercise: Entering Trance Through Touch

This has to do with the transfer of energy by the laying on of hands. What happens exactly is difficult to describe. Some feel as if a hot (or cool) stream was flowing through them, and others feel as if they are enveloped by clouds; still others speak of an electrical charge or of minimal movements within the body, as if the spinal discs were stretching themselves and breathing. Certain forms of touch can even take place over a distance, as in "long-distance healing." This is a form of spiritual healing in which mental energy is used to cause a healing change in a person through spiritual touch. Nonetheless, this kind of contact is often experienced physically. In the same way, thought seem to be able to take on some form of materialism so that it can be felt and is literally "hanging in air."

"Clair-feeling" (a term I have coined that is analogous to "clairvoyance") uses this ability of humans to get or be in contact, in some mysterious way, with the invisible and with things that are far away. Some people are so clair-feeling that everything moves them too deeply and they are unable to dissociate. Sensitivity and empathy, which are both important characteristics for a therapist, can be developed to such an extent that the person's own boundaries must be assiduously worked out and maintained. These people have a highly developed sense of atmosphere, vibrations, energies, and invisible forces, whereas others don't feel anything at all. Here, we are dealing with the transition to the areas of the supersensory.

Some people fall into trance merely by entering a room, a holy place, or the site of an incident. There seems to exist a certain kind of field of energy, whose effect, however, does not register on the average person. A slight massage—for example, stroking the forehead, fondling the neck, and so forth—can also put some people into a trancelike state, whereas it leaves others "unmoved" and is only experienced as somewhat relaxing or pleasant.

Certain areas of the body seem to be more suitable than others for altering the state of consciousness by being touched or manipulated. The neck is one such place. In the Terpsichore trance therapy, which was developed by Akstein and others in Brazil and is used in therapy, the neck is manipulated by slightly twisting the vertebrae. It is literally a twist of the head that induces an immediate trance in people practiced in this art. Because the twisting is performed while the person is standing up, the person can then be sent into a trance dance, which consists of letting uncontrolled impulses of movement "run free." This running free has a cathartic effect, and it can also be used for diagnostic purposes. The therapist can then see what really "moves" the patient. Later, the trance dancer can watch him- or herself on video and thereby become aware of the deeper motives of his or her behavior.

But if you find the running free to be too strenuous, as I do, and especially if it causes you to feel sick, you can just partake in the pleasant part of having the neck twisted and let a person you trust completely put you into a trance while lying down in a relaxed way. For example, I know a masseuse who can do this extremely well. As soon as she takes my head in her hands and moves it in a gentle figure eight, I fall into a very pleasurable, warm inner state. Then the world is okay again. My tensions dissolve, my breathing becomes deeper, and, from top to bottom, I feel integrated once more. It is as if at last streams of pleasant liveliness are able to flow again through the weak points of my tensed-up neck. Without running free, I find myself in a deep place, although I'm completely conscious.

In African and many other styles of dancing that would not necessarily be described as trance dance, you will find hurling, shaking, swaying back and forth, and backward and forward movements of the head, whose effects are similar to those achieved by the manipulation of the neck during trance dancing. But be careful! If you are stiff or otherwise unprepared, headaches or injuries can be the result of your boldness. Before you start, the neck muscles should be stretched a little. Then the vertebrae will not grind onto each other. Cracking noises generally indicate wear and tear, and shouldn't be caused more often than necessary.

Exercise: Entering Trance Through Movement

Similar to sleeping on something, there is the concept of taking a few turns around the block before making a decision, as if the physical movement of walking would change the decision in some way. Actually, walking does create a distance, both internal and external. The physical movement also changes our body chemistry. The "low point" is well known to joggers as a threshold, which, once it is overcome, leads to a "second wind." Breathing is now accompanied by a feeling of new, almost inexhaustible strength and a certain euphoria. Through the increase of muscle stimuli, the body's own hormones, the endorphins, which cause feelings of elation, are released. Of course, the better the condition we are in, the further this threshold is extended, which is why we always have to work harder and harder to reach the desired effect.

There are different types of trance dance. One way is based on simply overcoming the threshold and consists of dancing for hours on end. This can happen on a sacred plane as well as in the profane context of, say, teenagers dancing the night away in a disco. Dance halls used to be part and parcel of social life. In the late Middle Ages, the following excesses occurred that led to a ban on ecstatic dancing: As believers were put under increasing pressure to abandon ancient (heathen) customs and festivities, and submit to a regime of very strict piety, church services degenerated into wild orgies and blasphemies. Also, the carnival was used as a means of political protest and ended in bloody massacres. At the time when dancing was forbidden, because it was believed to be dangerous, depraved, and indecent, it gained a special attraction. The St. Vitus dances (erroneously named after St. Vitus, whose saint's day coincides with St. John's Day, or Midsummer's Day) were actually dance hysterics, which spread like epidemics. Reports about this dance have been documented and describe it as an uncontrolled shaking and trembling. There are indications of spasms, the cause of which has never been determined precisely.

Originally, the tarantella, a lively dance of southern Italy, was a trance dance. As legend has it, it was brought on by the bite of a tarantula spider, whose terrible pain could only be overcome by wild twitching and jumping. Musicians were called in immediately; their playing was supposed to prevent the bitten person from going insane. In this case, wild dancing seemed to be a way of dealing with pain. But soon it became obvious that the entire village was taking advantage of the situation and joining in, as their need to dance and let off steam appeared far greater than that during the usual festivities and parties. By virtue of being so exhausting, it made the dancers perspire and may have even put many into a trancelike state. And thus the transition from the wild fit to the controlled trance dance occurred.

In Africa and in some African-American enclaves as well as in Brazil, we find a similar distinction. A wild trance occurs when a spirit or a god takes hold of a person and possesses him or her outside the scope of the person's usual authority. This possession expresses itself in uncontrolled movements, which are described as dancing. If the person possessed gets the opportunity to express him- or herself ritually, the gods are pacified. They have found their sphere of activity, where they are understood and honored and their needs are fulfilled.

However, wild, uncontrolled possession is undesirable. The ritual provides a means of giving form to what is happening, and only then can it prove itself as truly healing. It is well known that dancing in trance can push a person to his or her extreme limits. The spirits who dance inside the person have no limits. Therefore, it is the ritual that has to set the limits. The ritual is for the good of the person—the spirits don't need it.

Even the dancing of the whirling dervishes looks controlled in its own way, and indeed it is. Whirling and turning around on one's own axis for hours requires a different sort of control than that needed for pirouettes performed by a ballerina, but nevertheless the spectacle you see shows no wild, unruly, and uncontrolled dynamics. Everything is specified and unwinds as if obeying eternal rules, like the movement of the stars, from which the dance of the Sufis is derived.

However, spinning as a kinesthetic trance induction is not limited to Islamic mystics. At a very early age, children love to experiment with circling and spinning movements. Their turned-up eyes show that they are losing their normal orientation, but they like doing this so much that when they fall down they get up right away and start spinning again. Worried remarks from adults—"Be careful so that you don't fall down!" or "That's going to make you sick!"—don't seem to deter them.

The waltz, which is derived from the turning movements of the *Ländler* (a German country dance), could have well evolved from the pleasure provided by spinning around.

Spinning on one's own axis is not the only way of circling. The fast, round dance that became exemplary in the mystic traditions of Hasidism causes the same effect of dizziness, only here it is not a single person or a couple that dances, but a group linked by holding hands. The rising momentum causes a fleeting balance. Somehow the pleasure and the ecstasy settle in through the collective movements, which keep the group together.

The last type of trance dance that I want to mention is the serpent form. Possibly it is the oldest form of all, as there are certainly numerous illustrations of it throughout history. The leading dancer is the head of the serpent—its consciousness, you might say. The other dancers, forming the body of the snake, often have their eyes closed and follow the leader, and can be said to represent the unconscious. The leading dancer is the moving force; he knows the way, and he also knows the solutions to many conflicts and problems that are dealt with ritually by the group during the dance. The dance out of the maze is one such dance. Processions led by a priest who gives a benediction demonstrate the same form.

Dance theorists have always pointed out the crucial difference between a controlled dance and a wild, uncontrolled fit of overwhelming pleasure or also of pain. The former is referred to as a "pictorial" dance, through which a meaning becomes clear, whereas the latter is called "un-pictorial." Here, nothing develops, apart from the pleasure of working the feelings involved out of one's system.

With or without a picture, the trance dance produces an effect of blissful exhaustion. And that's a benefit in itself, isn't it?

Trance Induction Through Hearing

The sense of hearing is assigned to the fifth chakra, which covers the parts of the body where the ears and the larynx are situated. The fifth chakra deals with expression and communication and with the intellectual processing of information, or thinking and understanding.

We distinguish between listening and hearing. Listening is a deliberate auditory perception, whereas hearing is a more widely spread and diffuse absorption of all kinds of different sounds that need to be translated into meaningful messages by the consciousness. Therefore, what we hear and what we do not hear are subject to a selective filtering.

Hearing refers to a continuity inside us that takes place in the unconscious. In the womb, we were able to hear our mother's heartbeat, and since then we have been receptive to rhythms that remind us of this time in our existence. Unlike seeing, hearing is not focused (focus comes from visual language). We can't choose whether we want to hear something or not, except by putting our hands over our ears, which reflects a certain biased attitude or expectation. The ears are openings in the body that have to be closed consciously, requiring a decision. The open ears we were given create an unbreakable and immediate connection to the outside world, which is constantly directing an assortment of information at us, whether it concerns us or not. Furthermore, the ears contain the organs of balance, which are responsible for our orientation in the world. They regulate our feeling for where we are automatically and without our conscious assistance. Our ears put us in touch with the world.

The word "absurd" contains the Latin word *surdus*, meaning "deaf" and "mute." It is a translation of the Arabic *jadr asamm*, which means "deaf root," and which in turn is a translation of the ancient Greek *alogos,* meaning "speechless" or "irrational."

Thus, hearing is strongly related to understanding, or, more precisely, the understanding of a language, and language is in turn related to thinking.

NLP distinguishes between two sorts of people, with differing means of auditory perception:

✧ **The auditory-tonal perception type** perceives noises just as they are, noticing the sound quality and the tone and all the background noises, before starting to think about their meaning; then he or she proceeds slowly to process the sensory impressions toward an interpretative conclusion.

✧ **The auditory-digital perception type** immediately translates everything that he or she hears digitally into meaning. Best suited for this is spoken language, which, however, can also be internalized. People in this category tend toward verbalization: They translate everything that they perceive and that reaches their consciousness into language.

The auditory-digital type is often found among intellectuals. Due to their academic education or a profession demanding constant definition and formulation of thought, intellectuals are forced to abstract quickly, and to distance themselves from the concrete, the sensory, and minor details, so as to gain from a distance a generic overview through generalization.

People in this category don't always say what they think, but their heads are like radios that never stop, constantly buzzing with comments, slogans, and suggestive messages. Negative affirmations may also be transmitted around the clock, such as "I'm a loser" . . . "I am never going

to make it" . . . "It's just no use." Positive affirmations, as developed through certain suggestive psychological techniques, endeavor to reprogram the auditory-digital type on this level by rewriting negative messages. These negative messages may result from a neurotic childhood and are replayed every day, thus maintaining the neurotic program. Positive affirmations promote a new program with simple slogans, such as "The world is a wonderful place" . . . "I am welcome here" . . . "I'll make it!"

However, if you are not an auditory-digital type and don't have much of a feeling for your inner monologue, for well-defined negative or positive sentences, and for language and thoughts in general, then all the trouble taken with positive affirmations will be a waste of time. Positive affirmations only work when other affirmations are already part of the program of the inner monologue. Intellectuals, however, often don't see why they should talk themselves into believing something that isn't true. And frequently they are not far enough advanced in their process of self-reflection to be able to perceive their own constant self-programming. Thus, positive affirmations should always be only a part of a therapy and should never be applied out of context, otherwise they just seem funny and elicit laughter or even cynicism.

Auditory digitalization is a relatively recent development in the history of evolution and is an ability that is typical of humans. Even if animals communicate with each other and have developed some kind of language, it can't be assumed that they use language to reproduce the outside world through an internalized model in a continual process of self-reflection. Only in this way, however, is thought possible. A prerequisite for thought is not only the ability to receive information, but also to store it and call it up again as needed, as well as to rearrange it in new combinations. These develop into the constructions that are responsible for brilliant inventions, imaginative works of creativity, and ethical ideas, but also for delusions, which have a system of their own.

In this connection, it is important to distinguish between

✧ felt emotions (the immediate sensory level), and

✧ understood emotions (the level of mediating by interpretation and meaning).

To start with, emotions are perceptions on the kinesthetic level. Then the auditory digitalization takes over and defines the emotions. This is not only a definition, but also an explanation as well as a fixation of the meaning found. The meaning is maintained through the name given to it. Conversational psychotherapy, which operates only on the level of speech and meaning, is therefore limited in its therapeutic effect. To bring about changes, it is advisable to shift to other sense channels and levels of perception (for example, supplementary body work).

Linguistic Metaphors

By way of practice, you can read these metaphors out loud—or if you are working in a group, you can read them to one another—listening for how they affect you.

✧ To talk big

✧ To talk till you're blue in the face

✧ To blare out

✧ To wag your tongue

✧ To have a sharp tongue

✧ To have an evil tongue

✧ To say something at the top of one's voice

✧ To shout something from the rooftops

✧ To tell somebody off

✧ To drum something into somebody

✧ To be deaf in one ear

✧ To be as deaf as a post

✧ That left me speechless

✧ Speechless with surprise

✧ To be only half listening

✧ That rang a bell

✧ This has a familiar ring

✧ That rings true

✧ To lend somebody one's ear

✧ To lend somebody a willing ear

✧ Loud colors

✧ To make a noise about something

✧ Deathly silence

✧ Silent as a grave

✧ To give your word on something

✧ By my word of honor!

✧ To break one's word

✧ To go in one ear and out the other

✧ To get an earful

✧ This sounds promising

✧ That caused an outcry

✧ To obey a voice

✧ The voice of the author

✧ To be called to do something

✧ To prick up your ears

✧ To change one's tune

✧ To strike a chord

✧ To make oneself heard

✧ The room has good vibrations

✧ It's music to my ears

✧ It struck a false note

✧ His voice had a note of desperation

✧ To notice a dissonance, or a discordant note

✧ To be in discord

✧ To be in accord

✧ That resonates with me

✧ To attune yourself

✧ To get a word in edgeways

✧ To have some say in the matter

Proverbs

"It's not what you say, but the way that you say it."

"God gave man two ears but only one mouth so that he hears twice as much as he speaks." This proverb, coined by the Stoic philosopher Epictetus, points out that obedience is worth more than self-expression through speech, especially in hierarchic structures of rule and control.

Exercise: Entering Trance Through Monotony

Always the same tone, the principle of monotony, can be applied to trance induction through hearing.

Monotonous rattling or drumming without rhythmic form or a supporting melody is one of the most common types of trance induction. It was customary in shamanism and is still used today, by Goodman and Harner, for example. The tempo is dictated not too fast but not too slow either, so that the individual notes can be distinguished from one another. The sensory listening experience conveys the impression of a kind of carpet of sound, which covers up the individual notes and combines them to form a single tone. The boundaries between the notes become blurred, veiling the consciousness like clouds of sound.

The principle of monotony and its astounding effect on the consciousness can be further explained by understanding the following: Our present-day wakeful consciousness, which has become the accepted norm of our everyday consciousness, has developed little by little over time. In the early stages of human evolution, our wakeful consciousness was nothing more than a state of increased vigilance. In this state, all sounds were evaluated as to whether or not they meant danger. If they were repeated, it was a sign that no disastrous consequences were expected. Vigilance had done its part and could switch off again, and a state of relaxation could ensue. The functions of the parasympathetic nervous system, like eating and digesting, could get back to work. But as soon as unknown noises reached the ear, vigilance was switched back on. We can observe this with animals that prick up their ears, even when they are eating, as soon as some noise attracts their attention.

This is why it is unhealthy to listen to loud sounds or exciting music during meals or times of digestion, like right before a siesta, or an afternoon nap. The wakeful consciousness still needs signals to turn off. One such signal for deep relaxation can be (although this doesn't apply to everyone) monotonous background noises.

The murmuring of a brook, the roaring of the sea, the rustling of a wheat field can all be a source of monotonous background noise. The bubbling that comes out of a synthesizer can achieve this effect artificially. Brain machines use these gentle and monotonous beats as an auditory stimulation, calming the wakeful consciousness and encouraging relaxation. It is only after a phase of such auditory stimulation that the visual stimuli from the glasses are added. The consciousness is now receptive and ready to accept the frequencies of the visual stimulus patterns, because our vigilance function is not expecting any sources of danger.

Monotonous rattling and drumming, on the other hand, doesn't have such a calming effect, but rather can cause a change in our consciousness. For most people, it is too loud and powerful in its sound quality to enable them to relax, let alone fall asleep. Indeed, sleep should not be the aim of a trance induction. Also, the sound quality should not satisfy aesthetic standards—it is not music. However, the person shaking the rattle or beating the drum should be able to hold an even beat over a certain period of time (and 15 minutes can be quite a long time). Each deviation from the evenness of monotony brings the immediate return of the wakeful consciousness. In addition, other disruptive noises, like that of the telephone, the doorbell, crying children (this is a special signal for every mother and pulls her out of an inner state immediately), or spoken words, are a message to the unconscious to listen and find out what is happening.

If a trance induction is spoken, the sound of the voice is crucial. The speech melody should not go from low to high, as in a question, but from high to low. A question is an appeal to the consciousness and jolts us out of a trance. Think about the way you react to these questions: "What do you want me to do?" . . . "Who do you mean?" . . . "What does it mean?" . . . "What's happening?" The language should be simple and precise, with clear instructions to the unconscious, which does exactly what it hears.

The unconscious doesn't understand abstractions, and so it doesn't know the word "not." If you give an instruction like "Do not smoke," it understands primarily "smoke"; the "not" is only recognized in a second attempt at information processing, by which time the unconscious has already prepared itself for smoking.

Although the instructions in a trance journey leading one back to happy childhood days, to a special sense of achievement, to a moment of fulfillment and peace, and so forth, should be precise, so that the wakeful consciousness doesn't have to ask itself what it is supposed to do, they should not specify exactly what such an experience of happiness, achievement, or peace consists of. For most of us, a description of waves crashing along the shore or gurgling water brings up associations having to do with a vacation and recreation. However, this is certainly not true for someone who once nearly drowned. Even happy childhood days can call forth very different associations. The instructions should be clear in their direction but leave the actual sensory experience open.

Such a trance induction could be the following: "And now let yourself go back in time as far as you think is right for you, and on the way back to your childhood, you may recall an experience that made you very happy at that time and still gives you a feeling of happiness today when you think of it." The unconscious starts searching straight away, and very soon it finds what it was looking for, because just hearing the word "happiness" already constitutes a suggestion.

It is always better to incorporate in your spoken trance induction (even if you are going to record the induction for yourself so that you can listen to it later on) the possibility that the suggested experience hasn't really happened but only exists in the person's imagination and desires. You can also refer to movies or even video clips and commercials. Everyone has experienced something at some time that represents happiness, be it a direct life experience or as indirect as a commercial recommending a particular product. The unconscious doesn't care where the information comes from—the important thing is that it's there.

By referring to the realm of desires, the activation of the wakeful consciousness is avoided, and with it the possibility that it may categorically reject being subjected to an experience of happiness in real life—especially if the identity of the person is tied up with being the eternally unlucky victim. "Happiness? Me? You must be kidding!" This puts an immediate end to the trance journey to possible happiness (an unlucky victim can alter his or her identity and suddenly become lucky, but, of course, only in

the future).

It goes without saying that when you are inducing a trance, you shouldn't stutter, crow, clear your throat, cough, or make slips of the tongue. Your voice should have the quality of a gentle lullaby and be kept in a low tone, and your words should be spoken slightly slower than usual.

Of course, we can think of counter-examples, like the inflammatory preaching voice of a Baptist minister, who talks himself and his congregation into ecstasy. But for normal therapeutic and personal use, such sermonizing is unsuitable, because it immediately stirs up memories of moralizing know-it-alls of all sorts. What's important in trance induction is for the person guiding the trance to give an impression of composure and openness, to convey neutrality, and to show an interest in the success of the trance. The best instructions sound as if they are spoken in passing, and they never convey the feeling of a fervent lecture.

Exercise: Entering Trance Through the Rhythm of the Heart

While still in the womb, we hear the blood pulsating and the rhythm of the heartbeat. And whenever we hear it again, we involuntarily enter a state in which we can recall our own origin. This may elicit feelings of apprehension and sentimentality, but also of excitement and stimulation, and of confirmation that we are alive. No auditory trance has such strong and immediate effects as the one that works with the rhythm of the heart.

The samba is a Brazilian dance that has this rhythm, and it causes Brazilians to dance through the streets at carnival time for days on end. The samba has three tempos: slow, for warming up; medium, more or less andante; and fast, in fact very fast, as we see brilliant dancers rotating their hips, whirling around, and letting their feet seemingly get tied up in knots, but never losing the rhythm. At demonstrations as well (for example, in 1990, on the occasion of the imprisonment of Nelson Mandela, who was released again shortly afterward), samba music is being used more and more. Nothing can surpass the rhythm of the heart when it comes to stirring up protests or creating an intense atmosphere.

Exercise: Entering Trance Through Playing Familiar Music

Older people are receptive to the music of their youth. That is why they often hire a pianist to play dance songs from the old days. Music elates and brings back into flow what has come to a standstill or has been forgotten with advancing years. Music mobilizes and provides access to lost memories. With age, and especially with diseases like Alzheimer's or senility, the short-term memory disappears and memories from early days emerge that the long-term memory has faithfully recorded and stored in pictorial form. When observing the fate of emigrants, I noticed what talking in the mother tongue can achieve: Through appropriate auditory stimulation, the whole person returns to a time when he or she felt at home and safe. Being reacquainted with one's mother tongue or hearing the hit tunes and slogans of a certain period creates a sense of familiarity that can hardly be replaced by anything else. Playing a hit from the time of their adolescence transports adults back into their youth.

Certain melodies catch our ear and awaken memories of the time when they were first heard. The melody is more important than the words, because it is etched deeply into our unconscious; the words are more or less interchangeable, as they first have to be translated digitally to obtain a meaning. We remember the first impression that the unconscious received of a situation when it heard a particular melody. If it was a pleasant situation, a pleasant impression will be associated with the melody for evermore. The composers of hymns sometimes made use of this effect, setting religious texts to well-known dance tunes. A hymn can also be enhanced when the pleasure of dancing is added to it. What were originally religious gospel songs are the soul hits of today, which transport the body spontaneously.

Exercise: Setting the Mood Through Singing or Humming

This doesn't mean virtuoso singing, which adheres to high standards of mastery for valid aesthetic expression. What is meant are those sounds that happen of their own accord. You may find yourself humming quietly, whistling enthusiastically, or singing in the shower. Or you may sing along in the last row of the church choir. What's important is that you open your mouth and something comes out.

It's the expression that is important. An expression for its own sake is meant here; the aim is not to please anyone but yourself. If you have learned to produce overtones, or harmonies, it's all the better. Perhaps you could add a few minutes of "toning" to the yoga exercises of your daily morning fitness program, not only letting your voice flow into the outside world but also granting yourself this special kind of self-massage. Notes are vibrations, and they let you vibrate. Not only do they apply to the outside world but also to your inside. You can reach your organs through the "holy notes" of Chinese medicine, but you can also revive yourself by simply singing or humming. Singing strengthens your breathing. You feel a slight tingling of the skin—this is a sign that you have started vibrating. And this inner vibration sets the right mood for trance. Try using your own personal instrument that is so well suited to the task: your voice!

Trance Induction by Connecting Auditory Stimulation with Digital Messages

As mentioned earlier, what's important is not so much what you say but the way you say it. The voice delivering the message is already part of the message. In the fifties, many advertisements were little ditties especially composed to catch the ear. When inducing a trance, be aware of the connection between the auditory stimulation and the verbal message.

Trance Induction Through Background Music

Constant background music, or Muzak, in public places, such as department stores, restaurants, and hotel foyers, is becoming more and more fashionable. One of the aims is to create a better mood in the customers so that they will spend more money. Music is used as a suggestive medium to mesmerize people or liven them up. But in some involuntary listeners, this can cause displeasure—not everyone likes to listen to a constant droning from morning till night.

Another use of background music is in music therapy, in which patients are subjected to specific sound waves. The vibrations of the tambura, a large gong, have proven to have especially healing qualities. Hearing strong, involuntary sounds, such as that of a gong, can cause an epileptic attack, which demonstrates that sound definitely has a real physical influence on the human organism. So be careful here!

Auditory Confusion Techniques

These are used chiefly in the trance techniques developed by Milton Erickson and in NLP. Two therapists speak to a client from either side, one in each ear. This method of trance induction seems to be very old, as Carlos Castaneda tells of having undergone a similar experience during his shamanistic training. Clients listen to something different with each ear, and they become confused, which brings about a change in their state of consciousness. Now they can hear everything, but the meaning of the messages is not the same as if they listened to them separately, one after the other. The simultaneity of the messages and their sensory overlapping change their meaning. A stereo effect of this kind can be achieved by listening simultaneously to two people, or when we have the TV and the radio switched on at the same time. If you put together two completely different messages from different channels, with different words or melodies, they form a unity conveying a new meaning.

The Dadaists were artists and writers who made up a movement based on deliberate irrationality and the negation of traditional artistic values, and they were the first to discover the aesthetic pleasure of consciously intended and voluntary confusion. They cut up texts and arbitrarily stuck them together again, forming text collages. They also put syllables together that didn't make auditory-digital sense, but produced a phonic, or auditory-tonal, composition.

The literal meaning of confusion is "flowing together," and this is exactly what happens when different auditory stimuli meet. But when the ear strives to make some kind of sense out of what it has heard, it sometimes manages to forge a new order instead of chaos, and that is the aesthetic attraction.

Auditory confusion techniques are also used to suggestively fix in the unconscious certain emotive words, like "happiness," "success," "optimum," and "excellent," and, in this way, attune the listener to their meaning, which is perceived casually and subliminally. Thus, two completely different stories can be told on a tape, both of which, however, include the emotive words uttered again and again in different contexts. These are then imprinted deeply on the mind and act as suggestions.

Polyrhythm as a Confusion Technique

We find polyrhythm first and foremost in the non-Western musical traditions of Africans, Asians, and Arabs. Polyrhythm simply means that various rhythms exist simultaneously and overlap one another. It is certainly not intended as a confusion technique, and a musician within any of these traditions would be insulted if polyrhythmical music were to be likened to chaos. Nevertheless, to unfamiliar Western ears, it often sounds like it. Polyrhythm is an order of such differentiation and complexity that it is not recognized by our rather simple Western ears, and we most certainly find it difficult to reproduce.

The practice of polyrhythmic structures is not only a wonderful training in chaos, but it also acquaints us with highly complex forms of order. Someone who claps, sings, stamps, swings his or her hips, and takes steps, while simultaneously playing a rattle, creating many different rhythms at the same time, will automatically leave the ordinary state of wakeful consciousness behind.

Yawning as an Exercise Before Auditory Trance Induction

Chaos can be translated as a "yawning abyss." Sometimes I experience the beginning of a trance as a buzzing in the ears and an impulse to yawn. Therefore, I deliberated whether or not yawning originally may have had something to do with trance and changed states of consciousness in general, which were described, in evolutionary terms, in dissociation from the relatively young wakeful consciousness, as chaotic conditions of the personal archaic past—and even gave chaos the name "yawning abyss."

I experimented with yawning, which is easily transferred as a reflex onto a whole group as soon as one person has started yawning. It became evident that yawning didn't always mean tiredness, but also produced it, in the desired form of pleasant relaxation.

Since then, I have used a yawning exercise as an entry into auditory trance induction before the rattling and the drumming or the gongs. The buzzing of the ears, caused by the yawning, can give you a foretaste of the slight disorders of balance that are associated with auditory trance induction. As the organs of balance are located within the ears, auditory experiences sometimes go hand in hand with kinesthetic changes, and vice versa. I move vigorously—for example, in a whirling dance—and I hear a murmuring, roaring, or buzzing in my ears. Many mystic experiences are described as auditory perceptions. Roaring, buzzing, thundering, and rumbling are the most well-known sounds. Of course, the inner voices that speak to people are auditory perceptions too. Discerning their origins and meanings is the task of the mind, which wants to understand correctly what it heard, but often finds it unfathomable.

Combined Forms of Trance Induction

The wish to be sensuous can lead to an unfortunate self-restriction. In our culture, sensuousness is limited too much to the realm of physical desires. It is the information that's important, and not necessarily the way it reaches us. Basking in the pleasures of the senses can easily become too much of a good thing if the process of information transfer gets stuck where it should only be at the beginning.

Synesthesia (literally, "joint perception"), as a mutual effort of all the senses, is a phenomenon that is considered to be a symptom of illness or an impediment, on the one hand, and an artistic talent or a sign of exceptional skills of perception, on the other. Mystics and poets have often described their experiences as synesthetic. The hearing of colors, the experience of sounds as if they were physical touches, the discernment of smells as if they were a taste in the mouth—these perceptions may not seem all that extraordinary even to us, because even in our everyday wakeful consciousness we are not always able to make distinctions among our sense channels. The stronger the experience, the more difficult it seems to be able to distinguish which of the senses has triggered the stimulus, delivered the message, or evoked the spell. Thus, the stronger the stimulus is, the stronger is the tendency to synesthesia. Under the influence of drugs, the synesthetic perception is strongest, because the sense channels are flooded. Such an overpowering experience makes distinction impossible and no longer allows us to speak about normal "sensuousness." Every physical notion is switched off, and the senses as functions become useless. Greater still is the euphoria resulting from "taking leave of your senses," or going beyond all senses.

Perception always involves a mixture. Pure perception types are very rare. The use of one investigatory sense channel is not sufficient to understand the richness of life. When we were very young, we learned to find our way in reality with the help of all our senses. Sensuousness is not only related to physical urges; it is also an instrument of intelligence.

In trance techniques, it is recommended to use a good mixture of all the senses. Methods that move from the generally accepted abstraction of the auditory-digital understanding (without which we would not even be able to finish elementary school or pass our driving test) to more archaic levels of perception in the history of evolution, like the kinesthetic sense of movement and touch, have proven to be particularly successful. Nietzsche, the German philosopher, recommended "letting the thoughts dance."

Understanding itself can be enlarged upon, if we take this literally. To actually stand in someone's place is more of an experience than just imagining it. In order to understand yourself and your problems better, and how they may be connected to certain conflicts, decision-making processes, or basic attitudes, try setting up these internal states as sculptures or reproducing them as a drama. This would entail transposing inner states to a sensory level of kinesthetic experiences through movement and touch, and thus experiencing them differently and undergoing a change, and then transposing them back to the original level, where you can interpret what happened.

Combined methods have also proven effective for anchoring and storing a successful learning experience in more than one sensory channel. This way, not only is the specific sequence of movements—for example, that necessary for riding a bicycle—memorized, but also the taste of success, my personal body odor, the brilliant colors that suddenly bathe the world, and the outer and the inner voices that confirm my success anchor the experience in me on a deep level. The more sensory channels that we appeal to and thus open, the stronger is the impression of what we experience. It is like the difference between mono and stereo, between black-and-white and color.

In trance, we are in a state of heightened receptivity anyway. This is why, in consciously induced trances, it is so important that everything be right: The smell of the air should be pleasant, the room should be a pleasure to look at, the clothing you are wearing should feel good against your skin, the taste in your mouth shouldn't remind you of anything indigestible or undigested, and the sounds should be chosen carefully. This also means that music should fade out slowly and not just be turned off. The loud clicking noise when a tape is switched off or the static crackling of a loudspeaker can turn the best trance into a flop. A good trance induction is like a successful multimedia show, and everything has to be carefully planned.

A tip to get the right taste in your mouth for trance: Eat light food and never go into trance on a full stomach. It's always better to travel light. I have noticed again and again that it was nearly impossible for my trance groups to reach ecstatic heights right after lunch.

PART II

TRADITIONS AND RITUALS

Ritual Trances

At a time when rituals still had significance and regulated people's lives, giving life meaning and helping people find their place in a higher order, it was common to go into trance before a ritual in order to experience the ritual in a heightened state. Otherwise, the process of intensive experience during the rituals could never have taken place. The ritual procedures are actually very simple. However, for someone not participating in the ritual, it is sometimes hard to grasp how these simple activities can cause such an exalted and holy event, as is the case with the Christian ritual of Holy Communion.

Freeing yourself from the everyday trance of habits is a prerequisite for entering the world where miracles can happen. In our culture, most rituals have become empty of significance, perhaps because they no longer evoke any enchantment. But in many other cultures, rituals still play an important role and are induced with a collective trance, which is socially accepted in religious contexts. Exhausting processions, pilgrimages, days of fasting, going without sleep, or other means of intoxication, make the transition from everyday life to the "other reality" easier. This other reality is actually always there, like a hidden side to our world, but only reveals itself occasionally and grants entry to those who are ready. That's why all traditional rituals are preceded by a fairly long period of preparation, the rules of which have to be followed diligently. This preparation serves to break through the patterns of habit, and thus also through the spell of the involuntary everyday trance, and it enhances existing expectations, which in themselves are a state of trance as well.

The more strictly the rules of preparation are adhered to, the more the ability to go into trance builds up by itself, so that outside aids, like drugs, are no longer necessary. Often enough, a mere signal of public permission is sufficient to put everyone present into trance, although nothing special has happened. I often witnessed this during charismatic church services. The general opinion that true trances are only possible through the effects of drugs, or are restricted to a few gifted people, is typical of a society that suffers from a lack of cohesion. Without cohesion, strong stimuli have to replace the dynamics caused by group energy, expectations, and faith (both sensory and supersensory), and a symbiotic solidarity.

The ritual trances described here are meant to encourage you to rediscover some place for the festive ritual in modern life. These ritual trances reflect a long tradition, but they are described in such a way that they can lead you on a journey of consciousness, as with meditation, into that "other reality." This means they can easily be used in everyday life. Each one in itself is a little celebration, which can be held daily, weekly, monthly, or on special occasions. Ritual trances are not only characterized by their careful preparation and their conscious induction, but also by their previously planned limitations. Trances can and should have an end. Thus, the trance is carried out in a ritual framework, which gives meaning and structure to what is happening and orientation and support to the traveler.

The ritual trances are ordered according to the elements. The sequence follows the order of the respective energy centers in the human body, and builds up from the bottom to the top. Following the ritual trances of water, earth, fire, and air are those having to do with space and time. This is where the transition from the ritual trance to meditation can take place. In this context, trance and meditation do not exclude each other, but are mutually dependent and build on each other. As the senses form the entranceway to the supersensory, dealing expertly and in a disciplined way with ritual trances can be the transition to a meditation that transcends the elements, as we perceive them in their abstract form.

Water Trances

Traditional Rituals and Customs

It can be said that life developed from a "primeval soup," because the evolution of all life forms began in the sea. The amniotic fluid in which the unborn baby floats is similar in composition to the water of the sea. Humans themselves consist to a large extent of water. Perhaps these are the reasons why the wish to return to one's origin is connected to the element of water. This yearning has a strong attraction. People always imagined *femmes fatales* as mermaids and water nymphs. The Greek god of the sea Poseidon, the elder brother of Zeus, was endowed with archaic powers and feared because of his ability to drive people insane. Archaic gods frequently appear as water serpents and dragons who live in the depths of the sea and are overcome and defeated by a hero.

In many myths, a water or sea goddess appears as a mother that replaces someone's real mother. Thus, for example, the sea goddess Thetis takes in Hephaistos after his mother,

Hera, rejected him and threw him out of heaven. The abandonment of newborn babies to the water is a frequent motif (take, for example, the story of Moses in the bulrushes), which could symbolize a surrender to the powers of water. Perhaps those rituals having to do with submitting to water, and especially the sea, have their origins there and confirm this original trust. In Bali, for example, the ashes of the dead are given up to the sea in a second burial ceremony.

The element of water is not only connected to life and birth, but also to dying and death. The river Styx, originally a goddess, flows through Hades, the ancient Greek realm of the shadows and the dead. It is this river that has to be crossed when the final break from life takes place and the veil of oblivion spreads across everything that has been experienced. Even today we say "to cross the Jordan" for dying. The ferryman is a mythic figure who leads human souls on their journey to the hereafter. People swore by the Styx (also a river connected to death and the underworld) and sealed the holy oath by drinking from the river. If the oath was false or was broken, water caused oblivion: The person fell into Lethe (another underworld river, whose name has given us the words "lethargy" and "lethal"), representing a state of sleeplike forgetfulness, which lasted a "great year" (approximately nine years). Possibly some of our profane rituals, such as celebrating something with champagne, are related to this form of taking an oath. In such myths, the element of water is also associated with the unconscious.

In addition, water is connected to fertility, birth, and regeneration. The Celts drank from a holy spring dedicated to a goddess of fertility or to the spring nymphs. The Christians often dedicated such healing springs to Mary, the Holy Mother of God. Waterfalls are holy places in many cultures. They are often the abodes of the gods of happiness and wealth (for example, in West African cultures). Our cornucopia, or horn of plenty, likewise pours out its benediction. The expression "to swim in money" is a metaphor for the liquefaction of real values into a stream of happiness. "Liquid" indicates wealth that is not property but can actually be used. But wealth that comes out of the water can also be deceptive and disappear from one day to the next.

Bathing in a healing well that regenerates and rejuvenates (for instance, the fountain of youth) is a motif of the late Middle Ages, whose bathing culture was only destroyed by the introduction of syphilis. Healing water plays an important role in myths and fairy tales: It often has to be fetched by a hero under great duress, and brings about recovery and deliverance. The myth of the Holy Grail as the holy chalice containing Christ's blood moves the subject on to the level of Christian redemption philosophy.

Baptism, in which a person is submerged in water or water is sprayed or poured over a person, is a Christian ritual modeled on the baptism of Jesus Christ by St. John the Baptist. Baptism is connected to giving a name or disclosing and sealing a new identity. Holy water is a means of protection, which preventively baptizes the believer again and again and confirms that he or she belongs to the chosen ones. Holy water is an effective weapon against the Devil in fairy tales and legends, and is also used in exorcism.

All kinds of washings have a ritual character. The cleansing before entering a mosque is one such ritual. Likewise, the symbolic act of washing one's hands of something, as done by Pontius Pilate, the Roman procurator of Judea, is an act of cleansing.

Are Water Trances Right for You?

Water trances have to do with liquefaction, and are recommended when

✧ you need to relax;

✧ you want to switch over from the stress of everyday life to a phase of recreation and leisure;

✧ you feel a need for withdrawal, seclusion, and absorption;

✧ the time has come for self-reflection and contact with your own feelings;

✧ the access to your own origin is blocked, and nothing moves you anymore;

✧ you question your identity and anticipate transformation;

✧ everyday life has become too narrow;

✧ your thinking has gotten stuck in a groove;

✧ your emotions are bottled up;

✧ there is a blockage in personality (inhibitions, grimness, etc.), which is physically felt and calls for a solution;

✧ beauty and grace are needed; or

✧ nothing flows or gains momentum by itself anymore.

These are most of the reasons that people try out trance in our rational times. They feel a yearning to get out of the rut of routine, out of the daily grind, and immerse themselves in a sea of possibilities.

Water trances should not be induced or precede working with other forms of trance when

✧ you perceive yourself as blurred, soft, bloated, overflowing with sympathy, flowing in all directions without limits, or flooded or boiling over with emotions;

✧ you feel yourself to be the slave of your pent-up emotions;

✧ the dam has already broken down, and you have not learned to deal with emotional outbursts, so there is a possibility of serious trauma or repressed shock;

✧ your personality structure is brittle, your ego is weak, and your boundaries have dissolved; or

✧ you like to swim with the current anyway, and thus will go under when the first difficulties arise.

In addition, depression, extreme introversion, and low blood pressure indicate that it is better to start with other trances to prevent a downhill spiral on all levels. Some people have difficulties in emerging again, and feel heavy, slow, dark, and locked into themselves after water trances. One training program that works with trances often starts with water trances to induce the necessary relaxation and offer an initial experience of the breaking down of boundaries. However, a training session should never conclude with a water trance.

Attune Yourself to Water

Align yourself with the element of water by letting your thoughts bubble over, spray, flow, drift, and stream, without any specific expectations, preconceived ideas, or interpretations. Repeat the word "water" in your thoughts, and let your visions, associations, memories, and sensory impressions come. Observe your feelings while doing this.

✧ Which forms of water in the list below are familiar to you and trigger emotions? What forms do these emotions take?

✦ A drop

✦ A spring

✦ A mountain brook

✦ A quiet lake

✦ A lagoon

✦ A swamp

✦ A beach

✦ The high seas

✧ Do you associate these different forms of water with memories of certain situations that have influenced and still do influence you? How do these memories feel?

✧ What feelings can you distinguish and name?

✧ What events are associated with these feelings?

✧ How do you feel in the element of water?

✧ What would you like to learn from the element of water?

Jot down your answers to these questions. They are important material for further work with water trances.

_____

_____

_____

_____

Position of the Body: Lying Down

You can help yourself become more attuned to the element of water by lying down. What's more, all positive experiences that you have with the element of water during your trance journey can be anchored in this body position and called up later in normal consciousness as required. Lying down evokes memories or associations having to do with being submerged in water, floating, or being carried by a stream.

✧ Lying down is the position in which the body gives in most to gravity, so it is the most relaxing of all body positions.

✧ Lying on one's back is often associated with the idea of being carried and transported by the liquid element. The swaying of a boat on gentle waves may remind you of being carried by your mother when you were a child or of being rocked in the cradle.

✧ Lying on one's stomach tends to evoke more of an association with active swimming or diving. The contact of the stomach with the ground that is bearing its weight can give you the feeling of being connected to the nourishing and supporting cosmos by some sort of invisible umbilical cord.

✧ Lying on the stomach with one leg drawn up is especially good if you have a backache, and is supposed to strengthen the kidneys. Sometimes merely relaxing the tensed-up back brings relief. The kidneys are organs of drainage that flush out the organism, ensuring a healthy water balance. When they fail to function properly, the sensitive balance of water in the body is disturbed.

✧ So, lying down in a relaxed way can lead to unconscious and immediate solutions to problems, if past trance experiences have strengthened your faith in your own depth, your unconscious.

Visualizations

✧ The purity of a spring

✧ The clearness of a pool

✧ The vastness of the sea

Affirmations

✧ To live means to be flowing.

✧ I let myself be carried by the great currents.

✧ I find my source, and draw strength and freshness from it.

✧ Water flushes me out and cleanses me of everything that is superfluous.

✧ Water renews me and keeps me young.

Trance Journeys

✧ Journey to the origin of the source of strength

✧ Bathing in a lake

✧ Diving down to the bottom of the sea

Trance for Refreshment and Renewal

Take some time for this trance every now and then. It won't take long, and will even give you the feeling that you have gained more time. Especially when you think you have no time at all, when deadlines are looming and everything seems to have gotten stuck, and you feel narrow and stiff and want to close up because the pressure has become unbearable, then the time has come to go into trance and turn reality from a solid into a liquid state.

Imagine or remember the wonderful, refreshing feeling of submerging yourself in a dark-blue or dark-green lake, of feeling the cool water on your skin and the weightlessness of your body. Then, when your head goes below the surface of the water, imagine discovering a world that moves at a slower pace, and is filled with dark secrets and surprises. Here, below the surface, you seem to glide without the usual efforts needed to move forward. Not only are your movements flowing and graceful and filled with natural beauty, but your way of thinking changes too, somehow becoming softer, as if it were about to dissolve and let you slip away into a dreamy state. Nothing is so terribly important anymore, and the hard facts of life take on a softer quality The more you let yourself drift, sink, or float, the closer you find yourself coming to solving your problems. You are in the middle of the lake of time. Time is nothing more than this flowing element that connects everything to everything else. Time flows through you and carries you further, just as the water carries your body.

Then, when you want to bring the trance to a conclusion, emerge slowly from your fantasies, from the dark-blue or dark-green waters, and go ashore by slowly sitting up—if you have been lying down—and letting your hands slip into your lap. With this gesture, you end the trance and fix in your mind the idea of letting everything unpleasant flow away. If you carry out this trance regularly and always associate it with this gesture, you will be reminded of it every time you put your hands in your lap. Everything superfluous flows away from you. New strength flows in. Everything is flowing. You will experience a feeling of refreshment, as if you had been far away for a long time, and can now approach the tasks facing you with new vitality and equanimity.

Everyday Rituals: Giving a Bath Greater Meaning

From time to time, allow yourself a bath (or a shower, or wash your hands if there is no opportunity for a bath or a shower) even if you are clean and don't need to wash. Look at this bath as a ritual that frees you of everything old that you don't need and supplies you with new strength. Or you could even consign to it the meaning of a baptism!

Set up your bath according to your personal preferences:

✧ Perhaps there is a special scent for the air that relaxes or stimulates you.

✧ You might want to choose a certain color and fill the bathroom with this light.

✧ Or you may prefer to listen to a certain piece of music, or just enjoy the silence.

Allow yourself to absorb the coolness or the warmth of the water, depending on your needs. As the water runs down your body, let everything flow away that is bothering you or plaguing you, that is too much for you, that is bottled up inside of you and putting you under pressure. Let it all go. Let everything flow away. Stop trying to hang on to things. Relax during your bath, and leave the bath like Venus, the Roman goddess of love and beauty, rising from the waves.

After drying your skin, complete the ritual by rubbing oil or cream into the skin to keep it soft and supple. At the same time, this activity-even if you do it all the time-emphasizes your personal boundaries. You need to protect the skin, your organ of contact. In fact, the skin is the largest organ of the body. It can be healthy and permeable, but also too thin or too coarse, or dried out and rough. Finish the ritual by doing something good for your skin.

Music for Water Trances

✧ Dark, soft sounds

✧ The most suitable instruments: horns, or wind instruments in general, and a full orchestra Falling cadences, minor keys, modulations from one key into another, so that you get the impression of floating through many layers and nuances

✧ Slow, rolling, constantly repeating rhythms, which form a flowing (not a staccato!), continuous sound

✧ Natural sounds of flowing, spraying, gurgling, and bubbling water, as well as the murmur of the sea or roaring breakers

✧ The voices of whales and dolphins

✧ Bubbling synthesizer sounds, and their echoes and reverberations

Further Tips

The room in which water trances are induced should be well heated, and you should be able to shut out the light. The floor covering should be warm and soft, and foam mats or mattresses should be available. The participants should wear comfortable clothing and warm socks and bring blankets and cushions with them, because in a water trance the blood pressure drops and the body and its extremities easily become cold. People whose hands tend to go numb are advised to bring an especially cozy blanket and gloves.

During the trance, the participants should under no circumstances be disturbed. That means no interruptions from other people, the telephone, the doorbell, or loud noises. Earplugs and eye masks could facilitate the trance.

Earth Trances

Traditional Rituals and Customs

It's said that God created man from a piece of clay. The element of earth represents the body and everything physical and material as well as visible and concrete. In psychotherapy, the term "grounded" not only has to do with accepting gravity, but also relates to being concrete and keeping "one's feet firmly planted on the earth." Earth stands for reality, form, and structure, for the practical things of life. At the same time, we attribute to the earth the ability to receive and store information. Many earth rituals are derived from this quality. Whereas water is connected to the unconscious and to sleep and dreams, the earth is associated with what has become real, including the real past and our memories of it. Ancestor cults are usually connected to the earth, by means of certain places or locations.

Prehistoric graves that have been excavated show the corpses lying in the same position as that of the embryo in the womb. In megalithic buildings, tiny chambers were discovered, into which a crouching person could just about fit. Even today, initiation rites still exist in which people withdraw into caves or let themselves be buried in order to return to the womb of the earth so that they can come out again reborn; thus, these little chambers may not have only had the function of a storeroom, but may also have been used for ritual purposes.

The Stone Age cave drawings show that caves were used as places of worship. Assemblies were held there, and the dead were buried there too. In this way, the spirits of the ancestors were present to advise their descendants and pass on their visions to them.

The healing sleep, which was popular in the ancient world, took place in a special place that may have originally been an area of natural energy and where the temple of a god with healing powers was subsequently erected (for example, the healing temple in Epidaurus, which is dedicated to Aesculapius). Statements of people in search of healing have come down to us over time. In the late Hellenistic period of ancient times, when more and more secret cults from the Orient were becoming established in the West, initiation rites took place in caves, or small underground rooms were built for the purpose, modeled on caves and tunnels. Every tunnel and every small room had a symbolic meaning and corresponded to a period of transformation.

Prehistoric marks of a holy path in winding but well-ordered tracks, which either led up a hill in a spiral or formed a pattern of circles and spirals on level ground, have been interpreted as a calendar or as tracks laid down for ritual movements.

Processions and pilgrimages to holy or consecrated places were also adopted by the Christians. Examples include climbing a mountain under difficult conditions, shuffling along on one's knees (St. Patrick in Ireland), as well as the arduous approach to the inner sanctum across many steps or extensive grounds.

The ritual walking around a place ("circumambulating") is also known. It originally had the magical effect of circling and later evolved into a gesture of reverence and humility. The slow approach could also be interpreted as a preparation for entering the place of power. The origin of covered walks and cloisters may well go back to the pattern of ritual preparation and attunement through slow walking.

Lying stretched out facedown on the floor is part of the Christian ordination ceremony for nuns and monks. This practice may be more than just a gesture of humility, as its origin may lie in an archaic reverence for the earth.

The oracles of ancient times resided in caves (Cumae) or near ravines (Delphi). Being close to the earth seems to endow humans with super-sensory knowledge. Fumes and radiation may also have played a role in inducing the trance that the priestesses were in when they uttered their prophecies. Today, there are still caves in Togo in West Africa that are dedicated to the earth goddess Nana. It is said that in these caves you either learn to speak in a thousand languages or you go insane.

In the African-American obsession cult of voodoo, there is a kind of oracle on which the signs of the gods are drawn in an orbit, indicating their different locations. The place where the dancer falls to the floor in trance is a sign of which *voduns* (West African gods) he belongs to. The drawing of magic circles and signs also plays an important role in Western magic.

The labyrinth in Crete was originally a natural cave or a mine. According to mythology, taking the winding underground paths as a model, the genius Daedalus designed the labyrinth, which you can still see today in the ruins of the palace of Knossos. The labyrinth was the dwelling place of the monster Minotaur, which fed on people. It was vanquished by the hero Theseus, who freed the Minotaur's victims and put an end to the sacrifices. But the labyrinth remained a symbol for initiation, which can also be seen in illustrations of the Christian Middle Ages. Theseus represented Christ and the Minotaur the Devil. Christ defeats the dark inside the earth, brings supernatural light, and leads the souls that are imprisoned in the dark out of the prison of this transitory life. Here, earth is reduced to the status of being "only worldly."

In the Christian burial ceremony, the body is given back to the element earth with the words: "Dust to dust, ashes to ashes, earth to earth."

The earth takes up the mortal remains. Thus, it becomes a vessel and a receptacle for what is mortal, while the immortal soul separates from the body and frees itself. The body was often looked upon as the prison of the soul. This idea is reflected, for example, in Plato's cave parable. But in esoteric traditions, the body is seen as a temple and is cared for. It evokes ideas of a holy room, a building in the form of towers or temples, and the Holy City.

The rituals of ordering and orientation are associated with foundation rituals. In ancient Sumer, the kingdom had to be founded anew by the king at the beginning of every year, and he had to defend it against the destructive powers of the primeval serpent, which was ritually cut into pieces. The city was laid out according to the directions of the four winds, and at the center of the cross a phallic rod was erected that rose out of the earth and symbolized the center of the universe.

The ritual cutting up of the primeval serpent can be found in many traditions. In certain fertility rites, the pieces of the serpent are buried (refer to the Hainuwele myth of Borneo). The practice of burial in which one is buried alive or immured seems to still have occurred in native customs up to the modern age. In the Alps, there used to be a horrendous custom in which a simpleton was made king for one day and all his wishes were fulfilled, after which he was stoned to death and buried under a pile of stones. This is the origin of the expression "buried wishes." In foundation rituals, a cornerstone was often laid, under which a sacrificial animal was then buried, and other horrid legends even tell of mixing mortar with human blood.

Erecting oversized buildings—such as the pyramids in Egypt and pre-Columbian America, and the modern buildings in many big cities today—can be considered an attempt by man to put up a monument to himself in order to overcome his mortality. The building of monuments in particular is one way of giving solid and lasting form to our transient history.

Are Earth Trances Right for You?

Earth trances have to do with reinforcement, and are recommended when

✧ you feel a need to ground or anchor yourself;

✧ you are looking for something to hold on to, for structure or orientation;

✧ the time has come for self-determination and contact with your personal claims;

✧ the ego wants to settle and take on form, wants to achieve something in life;

✧ the consciousness orients itself around tasks, duties, and achievements, but also around possible success, and needs the support of the unconscious to do this;

✧ some kind of foundation lies ahead, and the ground has to be prepared;

✧ the ground seems to be sliding from underneath your feet, or you have lost it already; or

✧ chaos looms as a bottomless ravine, and the need for security is predominant.

Most of the above are the reasons that many people believe order can be achieved by reason and common sense alone. All too often, people relinquish the powers that the earth can bestow on them if only they are willing to go into trance. Earth trances are often used after water trances to "solidify," reinforce, and anchor the new experiences that came about through the contact with the unconscious.

Earth trances should not be induced when

✧ you are stuck on old patterns and habits,

✧ you adhere stubbornly and defiantly to your judgments and opinions, or

✧ you have "closed the door" on life, and cannot be moved or surprised by anything.

Earth trances have an integrating effect. But, of course, there needs to be material that can be worked with and integrated. If you are unwilling or unable to look at yourself and imagine new possibilities, you will have difficulties with earth trances, because the armor of a closed or a hardened attitude cannot be sufficiently dismantled. In cases like this, nothing new can be taken in. The earth has an absorbing effect, especially when it comes to healing. Earth trances are therefore particularly suitable for concluding a trance program.

Attune Yourself to the Earth

Attune yourself to the element of earth by letting your thoughts find a way forward, step by step in a kind of procession, without preconceived ideas, classifications, and interpretations. Your thoughts lead you from one impression to the next, leaving a structure or a trail that not only tells you what you have thought but also how you have thought it. The earth stores everything and bears witness to it. Repeat in your mind the word "earth," and let the visions, associations, memories, and sensory impressions arise. Pay attention to the effect this has on you, observing the consequences as if you were following a trail. Draw conclusions and then take stock. Pay special attention to your immediate physical sensations.

✧ What happens in your body when you imagine the following transitions:

◆ from water to earth, for example, when stepping on firm ground after taking a bath, sailing a boat, or walking across a swamp or a frozen area;

◆ from air to earth, for example, through a secure landing after a plane trip, or when coming down to level ground from great heights;

◆ from unknown territory to familiar surroundings;

◆ from wilderness or desert to developed, cultivated, and fertile land;

◆ from frozen and bleak winter earth to the first signs of life and the activities of nature as it prepares for spring;

◆ from the earth full of secrets, treasures, and powers to a wasteland of rubble; and,

◆ in a change of perspective, from the earth as a solid element to the earth as a planet.

✧ Are you able to assign different feelings to the transitions described above? What are these feelings?

✧ Can you distinguish which feelings are pleasant and which are unpleasant?

✧ Are there situations in your daily life that are comparable to these transitions and the emotions that they evoke in you?

✧ What changes would be necessary in your everyday life to let the pleasant emotions prevail?

✧ And what would be the conditions for such changes?

✧ What would you like to learn from the element of earth?

Make some notes. This is important material for your further work with earth trances.

_____

_____

_____

_____

Position of the Body: Crouching

You can help yourself become attuned to the element of earth by adopting a crouching, or squatting, position, or the position of the embryo in the womb. In addition, all the positive experiences you have had with the element earth on your trance journeys can be fixed in your mind while you are in this position and be called up immediately in everyday life as required. The crouching position takes the head, hands, and feet out of contact with the outside world and the periphery, directing them to the inside, to the middle of the body, and by so doing facilitates concentration. The body openings as well seem to close off to the outside. Through the act of drawing your limbs together and rolling yourself up, you can fully focus your attention on the inside. Crouching is a position of protection, of turning away from the outside in order to concentrate completely on yourself and steer all powers toward yourself, but it is also a position of preparation and waiting,

Crouching has a calming effect in cases of shock and pain, and is adopted involuntarily when the demands of the outside world become too great. That is why it is often associated with phases of regression. However, the aim is to allow ourselves these times of self-protection when we need them, re-emerging into the outside slowly and when we are ready, and taking up contact again when we feel the time is right. Although physical contact and touch can inspire trust, they can also be threatening and disturbing. Therefore, as a therapist or a group leader, you have to be sensitive to be able to recognize the needs of other people.

Visualizations

✧ Your own physical body (outline)

✧ Your own mortality (burial)

✧ Erecting a monument to yourself (legacy)

Affirmations

✧ The solid form of my body with its outline shows me my identity and integrity.

✧ The thought of my own transience and mortality gives me determination.

✧ The present is the place of greatest strength. I am in contact with the earth that carries me.

✧ Everything I do derives its meaning from what I leave to the world—in whatever form and at whatever time.

Trance Journeys

✧ Journey along gravity to the inside of the earth

✧ Journey to the natural resources and your own potential

✧ The personal oracle (finding the right place)

Trance: Coming Home

Every now and then, take some time to go into this trance, especially if you are feeling indecisive, confused, and uprooted, as if you had lost the ground from under your feet. Give your "inner home" a chance to find you.

Imagine or remember setting your feet down on the ground somewhere, coming into a country, seeing a landscape, or finding a place for yourself that immediately made you feel at home. Imagine or remember letting yourself settle in, allowing all the tension to flow out of you, breathing a long sigh of relief and with it shedding all the foregoing strain and confusion, all the hustle and bustle, and feeling like you had finally arrived.

Finally you are where you had always wanted to be. Allow this feeling to spread through your body, and let yourself feel grounded, especially in the parts of the body that are in contact with the floor. Whether you are lying down, sitting, or standing, give in to gravity. Grant yourself this relaxation, and thereby reinforce the feeling of certainty that you are in the right place. Experience this feeling of security and trust right now. Become aware of the contact with the ground or the seat you are sitting on. Don't search with too much intensity or effort. Just let the ground find you, take you up, and keep you. Picture setting yourself down like a piece of luggage that is too heavy to hold. Remain like this for a while.

Then conclude the trance by stroking the outline of your body and becoming conscious once more of the solid form of your presence in the here and now. In this way, you anchor the feeling of having arrived and will retain a sense of self-assurance even in moments of hectic activity.

Everyday Rituals: Visiting Your Personal Place of Strength

For this ritual, don't choose a place that is difficult to get to and that you can only visit from time to time. You need a place that you can retire to any time, a special place in your house, in your garden, or in your immediate surroundings. It doesn't necessarily have to be outside—especially if you don't like drafts, insects, or humidity. Choose a place where you feel relaxed and at home. For most people, this is their own bed, the sofa, or a deck chair on the balcony, but it can also be the corner of a room set up for meditation. The ritual, which you should perform daily, simply consists of visiting this place very consciously and realizing: Here I have arrived, here I am at home, here I am secure, here I am now, here I am completely in contact with the supporting ground. Even if this ground is only rented, this is the ground on which I collect myself. It is my home, my native territory.

Leave behind the tension of everyday life with its harassment, confusions, uncertainties, and worries, and concentrate fully on the physical sensations of pleasant heaviness and unity. Let your breath become calm, shed your worries, and confirm the harmony and the unity of your life at this moment. Observe your breath as it becomes deeper and calmer, and allow yourself the certainty that you are here, which gives you a feeling of security and self-assurance. Go completely into yourself, and stay for a while at that spot where you can feel your own center, permitting a feeling of relaxed, calm self-control to grow inside of you. Here, you are the master of the house!

Then conclude the ritual with one last deep breath, assuring yourself one more time that you are secure and supported. Perhaps you will now experience a feeling of gratitude, and will want

112

to end the ritual with some words like "Thank God!" This way, the feeling of gratitude will be anchored inside of you and will support you whenever you need it.

Music for Earth Trances

✧ Traditional drum music from Africa, Australia, and the North and South American indigenous cultures

✧ Clearly structured music in harmoniously proportioned phrases, as in the court music of the baroque period

✧ Music that is suitable for slow, graceful dances, processions, and round dances, and has no great variations in rhythm and tempo

✧ Music with four-beat time, or good for marching

✧ Dark, deep drumming notes, basses

✧ The Australian instrument didgeridoo, the Tibetan ragdong

✧ Deep singing voices

✧ The deep notes produced by a synthesizer

Further Tips

The best locations for holding earth trances are suitable places in nature, such as caves and ravines but also meadows and hills in the open countryside. But take a mat or something that you can lie or crouch down on comfortably, as well as a blanket or a sleeping bag as a protection against cold or humidity, insects, thorns, disturbing light, and so forth. Maybe you have a special ritual blanket for meditation. Bring a sufficient supply of bottled water, and perhaps some hot tea in a thermos, as well as some food for getting back your strength afterward. Photos of the location where the trance took place can serve as a memento, and the exact coordinates of the place on a map will help you find it again.

In an enclosed room, the cave character should be emphasized, and everyone should have enough time to find a suitable place to situate him- or herself: Corners, niches, or edges are best.

Fire Trances

Traditional Rituals and Customs

Many myths tell of man's achievements having to do with creating and using fire. These myths often entail a heroic deed, when a person or a demigod asserted himself against the forces of nature or the gods. For example, in Greek mythology, there's the story of Prometheus, who brought fire from heaven to man, and was punished for it by Zeus. In one West African myth, man exchanged his own immortality for fire: He asserted his will and won fire, but in so doing became mortal.

Rites and customs make us aware that fire has to be maintained, cared for, and constantly re-lit if we want to keep this valuable gift that we fought so hard to obtain. Lighting a fire is a ritual in some places on Easter night, and Jews celebrate the holiday of Chanukah by lighting candles in a minorah. Another ritual involves donating a candle, which is ritually lit in connection with a certain request and set up before the altar. In a West African ritual dedicated to the fire god Shango, the person possessed by Shango goes from house to house carrying a fire in a calabash on his head. And there's the eternal fire of the Olympic torch. Torch processions have a long history. In one legend, the hero who defeated the darkness carried the torch as a sign of triumph. Under the Third Reich in Germany, archaic rites were revived, including torch processions and monumental light shows, where floodlights were used to induce mass trances.

Maintaining the valuable fire, which used to be such a lengthy process to light, was especially important in times when fire was often the only protection against the cold, darkness, and wild beasts. Humans went from guarding the open fire to watching the fire in the hearth. In the home, the fire became the responsibility of the women, whose domain was there. The Roman vestal virgins were priestesses of the fire in the sacred hearth. The witches of the Middle Ages called upon their helping spirits near the stove or the open fire, which thus became the point of entry for air spirits.

Normally, when you touch fire directly, you burn yourself. However, in the exceptional state of trance, people have been known to touch burning coals, put them in their mouths, and walk upon them. Walking on fire has its origins in healing ceremonies in which the will of the mind overcame the forces of nature. The Orthodox Christians of Greece have kept up the tradition of walking across fire to this day.

There are customs that involve dancing in and around a fire. In the Alps, for example, on Midsummer's Day, young women and men jump through the fire together. If the couple holds hands and doesn't let go, the relationship is said to be lasting.

Fire not only provides light and warmth; it's also meant to have a cleansing effect. In the Middle Ages, the stakes that were built for heretics and witches, in order to burn them alive, also had the macabre function of freeing the immortal soul from worldly sins.

Purgatory is a place of purification. The flames of damnation, as shown in medieval illustrations, have the effect of a cleansing fever that burns away all impurities.

The burning heart of Jesus is a symbol for limitless sympathy. The mystical unification with God is often described as a consuming flame. This was experienced by the mystic Theresa of Avila and is part of Islamic Sufi mysticism.

The blazing flame overcomes gravity and rises up toward the sky. That's why the flame is a symbol of the human striving for higher things and the human longing for greatness and eternity.

Fire trances have an ecstatic character, and are practiced especially by people who feel drawn toward the element of fire. They love taking risks and are ready for total commitment. But also for those who are not so fiery by nature, a fire trance not only can be a huge challenge, but can also provide great inner benefits, because it revives the inner fire, sexuality, and *joie de vivre*. However, this is only so if the trance has been well prepared for and is the result of one's own decision. Otherwise, encountering the inner fire can be overwhelming, becoming a threat or even a shock, and can spoil an interest in trance experiences in general.

Fire trances should not be induced
✧ when you are in an extreme state of exhaustion,

✧ if you have had a traumatic sexual experience, or

✧ if the challenge of the trance has to do with a demand for achievement or with proving your own worth through a test of courage, because both will distract you from yourself rather than lead you toward it.

Furthermore, high blood pressure and heart problems are signs that you should not put yourself under this pressure; instead, move into trance slowly step by step after a warming-up phase, and let the trance intensify gradually. A fire trance with its ecstatic climax should always be followed by a closing phase, to round off what transpired and let the trance come to an end gently. It is important to come down and cool off, to convert the fever into a normal temperature.

Are Fire Trances Right for You?

Fire trances are related to enthusiasm, and they are recommended

✧ for the expression of passion;

✧ to kindle a fighting spirit;

✧ when your urges make you feel restless and demand some kind of climax;

✧ when there is a danger that the inner dynamics will flare up, and this force needs to be converted into outer movement;

✧ when you want to experience extreme states, ecstasies, and excesses within a protected and secure framework;

✧ when the time has come to put all your energy into a high ideal and to commit yourself completely to this;

✧ when a process of cleansing and purification is called for;

✧ when radical and revolutionary changes are due; or

✧ when the inner fire has died down or gone out—for example, through reduced vitality, weakened health, lack of drive, inhibited sexuality, or general lack of enthusiasm.

Attune Yourself to Fire

Bring yourself into accord with the element of fire by letting your thoughts flare up, heat up, start burning like a straw fire, spread like a wildfire, and shine like a light in the dark, without any particular preconceived ideas or interpretations. Repeat the word "fire" in your mind, and allow visions, associations, memories, and sensory impressions to arise. Pay attention to which of these especially spark your interest.

✧ Which forms of fire in the list below kindle your passion and enthusiasm the most? Try not to be influenced by moral judgments of good or bad and benefit or harm.

◆ Erupting tongues of fire

◆ A spark

◆ A flame that suddenly flares up

◆ A wildfire that spreads quickly

◆ A hearth fire, emitting constant warmth

◆ An extensive fire that burns down everything around it

◆ Smoldering embers

◆ A red, glowing lava stream

◆ The fire of the Apocalypse

◆ The bluish, cold light of electrical charges

✧ With which form do you identify the most?

✧ And which physical sensations, emotions, and thoughts does such identification evoke?

✧ What does the element of fire mean to you, and how do you create your own inner fire?

✧ What would happen if you let your inner fire be more predominant in your everyday life or gave it another form?

✧ What consequences would this have, especially as far as your relationships are concerned?

✧ What would you like to learn from the element of fire?

Jot down your answers here. They will provide important material for further work with fire trances.

_____

_____

_____

_____

Position of the Body: Standing

You can help yourself get into the right frame of mind for the element of fire by standing. But standing like a rising flame, defying gravity, differs from the normal way of standing. Try standing on your toes like a ballerina and letting the tension that rises up engulf the whole body. Stretch your arms up above your head until they seem to grow into the air, and then stretch out your fingers as if you wanted to pull the stars right down out of the sky. Whenever you feel like a rising flame while you are standing, you can call up every positive experience you have had with the element of fire in your trance journeys, which you anchored in this standing position, so that you can use the powers you gained immediately any time you need them.

Visualizations

✧ Lighting the inner fire

✧ Keeping the inner fire

✧ Transferring the inner fire

Affirmations

✧ I have got fire.

✧ My inner fire makes me feel warm and shines through me.

✧ My inner fire can always be re-lit, and I know how to do it.

✧ My inner fire can enthrall other people.

✧ When I rouse my inner fire, I become one with myself.

✧ When I feel enthusiastic about something, my inner fire begins to glow.

✧ When I let my light shine, I love myself and everything with which I come into contact.

Trance: Kindling the Inner Fire

Take some time every now and then to carry out this trance, especially if you are feeling down or resigned, or don't find life worth living anymore. Take the time to give your inner fire a chance to flare up again and take hold of you.

Imagine or remember the eyes of someone who loves and desires you. Picture these eyes looking at you so passionately that they have a feverish radiance. In response to this wild, demanding, and fiery look, you feel heat rising up inside of you. Allow this feeling of inner heat to spread, to fully engulf you. Now breathe deeply to experience even more heat, more radiance, more passion. Breathe into your solar plexus so that it relaxes you; at the same time, feel how your breath becomes deeper and perhaps faster, and allow this passionate breathing to put your body into a state of inner movement. Then place your hands on your heart and let your heart open wide, so that the excitement can rise and take hold of your heart, filling it with light and warmth, and making it shine.

Let yourself fully experience this fire inside of you, and feel how it spreads and wants to engulf everything around you, far beyond the limits of your own body, your own skin. Feel how the fire puts you into contact with your own generosity, even if your heart felt small and mean before. Now move your hands away from your heart and extend them into the room.

Stay like this for a while, savoring the new space you have embraced. Then, when you feel that this experience of generosity is well anchored inside of you, put your hands back onto your heart and press them there, so as to keep the inner fire aglow in your heart. Be sure to end this exercise very consciously with the closing of the heart space, which is not a locking up but rather a conscious gesture expressing limits.

If you have difficulty bringing up from your memories or imagination the image of someone looking at you this way, just pretend you are in one of those romantic, sentimental movies, and some famous actor or actress is looking at you with eyes ablaze with desire. Even if you would not normally watch a movie like this, give it a try. As the actor or actress looks at you with wild, blazing eyes, allow yourself to swoon and catch on fire. If you find this embarrassing, you don't have to tell anyone about it.

Everyday Rituals: Experiencing the Fever of a Challenge

Today, we know that having a fever has a healing effect. However, some people hardly ever have a high temperature. Nonetheless, all of us can integrate this ritual into our everyday lives if we allow ourselves to get into a sweat every now and then. This can happen when you are climbing stairs or engaging in some sport, but also when you find yourself in a situation that is unusual for you and that is in some way a challenge. Overcome your reluctance and permit the inner excitement to build. Feel the inner heat, the slight tingling of the skin, perhaps a shaking of the knees. Feel the heat of a challenge, and let this become a ritual. This challenge can be the overcoming of shyness but also of indecisiveness, lethargy, or resignation. Allow yourself to show involvement—even if it is only with yourself. Allow your inner fire to put you into a fever every now and then. Always end the ritual with the gesture of placing your hands on your heart, so that the flame of your heart will be protected and preserved.

Music for Fire Trances

✧ Swaying, rolling rhythms

✧ Music to three-beat time

✧ Music with rhythmic acceleration

✧ Stimulating rhythms

✧ Percussion instruments, especially drums

✧ Music in which the dynamics build up slowly

✧ Traditional music from Arabic cultures

✧ Indian ragas that start slowly and end in a wild climax

✧ African and African-American music with a fast, driving beat

Further Tips

During a fire trance, the room should be decorated festively and colorfully; try using flowers, beautiful gowns, material with exciting patterns, and scents to spark the atmosphere. The room should be well heated in order to support the starting phase of warming up. Clothing should be in layers so that pieces can be taken off and put back on as needed, and it should enhance your beauty—no baggy jogging suits! A touch of the erotic helps to let the inner fire flare up.

Air Trances

Traditional Rituals and Customs

Some creation myths tell of a time when there was neither air nor space in the world. In one such myth, our ancestors lay close together, entwined around one another, and it wasn't until children were born from this union that a problem arose: The children needed space and air to breathe. So the children started to crowd into their living space and to push their parents apart. That's how space was created for humans, and it is here that they are at home and have air. In this myth, the element of air is associated with the destruction of the primal unity that was necessary for humans to develop. At the same time, air is also an element that holds all of us together. Another creation myth describes how the dawn was impregnated by a wisp of wind and gave birth to the very first egg. Traditional rituals in particular stress the combining, informing, and inspiring character of air. Messages are entrusted to the wind, which carries them further or sends them up to the gods.

Smoking rituals endeavor to send signs. The smoking of the peace pipe unites the circle of those present and strengthens their mutual decision to make or keep peace. Cain felt envious of Abel's smoke signal that went straight up to the heavens, while his own fire just smoldered and the smoke wouldn't rise into the sky.

Requests and wishes can be transmitted by writing them down on paper and then hanging up these pieces of paper so that the air can take them away. This is the idea behind decorating trees with ribbons and pennants. Tibetan Buddhist prayer flags have a similar purpose. These flags have sacred texts written on them or bear pictures of holy figures, so when they come in contact with the air their messages are reinforced and spread.

Pennants and flags are used to keep away evil spirits and attract good ones. Totem poles outside the houses and settlements of the Native Americans of the Northwest serve the same purpose, and are also visible from afar and mark the inhabited territory.

In modern times, flags and banners are still important. An oath is sworn on the flag, and a flag is placed over the coffins of fallen soldiers. Hoisting a flag is an international sign of victory and taking possession.

Wind chimes, called *caccia spiriti* (literally, "spirit chasers") in Italy, are hung from trees or the entrances of houses to keep away evil spirits. You can also find such wind chimes outside the Buddhist temples in Japan.

In some Native American traditions, "dream catchers" are strung up on round frames and hung beside the bed. These netlike objects are supposed to let only the good dreams through, while keeping the bad dreams at bay.

As a sign of liberation, song birds, kept especially for this ritual purpose, are released from their cages and literally thrown into the air. I know this custom from Nepal as well as from the south of Italy. In both cases, it is associated with the wish for personal freedom and is said to bring good luck.

There is a ritual in which the ashes of the dead are scattered to the four winds to completely extinguish their existence, including their past and their future. In many cultures, it is believed that the deceased, when buried in consecrated or native earth, are taken up by it, but when in contact with the element of air, are subjected to a kind of dispersal from which they never recover.

Are Air Trances Right for You?

These trances are hardly recognizable as such. Still, scientific research into the condition of the brain waves during these trances have shown that it is different from that in normal states of consciousness: Instead of the usual beta waves, alpha waves are measured. All mental states developed in yoga or modern mind control (for instance, Silva Mind Control) lead to a similar condition of changed consciousness. Trance is the basis for new ways of thinking, learning, and communicating, and air trances, as described here, can be a good start.

Air trances pertain to liberation, and are recommended when you

✧ want to gain distance from everything,

✧ are ready to look at the world in a playful way and take things easy,

✧ wish for more freedom and space, or

✧ want to increase your ability to think and learn.

Air trances should not be induced when

✧ you, as a result of your predisposition or your profession (computer, for example), are "inside your own head" too much;

✧ you are overstimulated, or "overcharged," and possibly not grounded enough due to your constitution or your personal situation;

✧ the danger exists of "taking off," "freaking out," or getting entangled in delusions, wild thoughts, or philosophic or esoteric theories, and not being able to come back down to earth;

✧ you have difficulties concentrating;

✧ thinking and learning tasks exert excessive pressure on you; or

✧ your intelligence is weakened or underdeveloped (due to drugs, mental retardation, learning disorders, or difficulties concentrating due to social factors).

These contraindications, however, only apply to advanced air trance techniques, which are not mentioned here. They deal with confusion, chaos, and paradoxes. Polyrhythm can be an important introduction to such trances (for example, Reinhard Flatischler's Ta-Ke-Ti-Na method).

Air trances complement a training program that aims at constructively using and applying trance in everyday life. In school, in creative and intuition training, and in the search for vision, they are an excellent means of induction that promote intelligence in a light and playful way. At the same time, they awaken pleasure in thinking and disprove all misguided ideas that have to do with trance dulling the mind and making one stupid. However, because trances are based on a state of deep relaxation and a calm and unintentional disposition, it is important to create a light and playful atmosphere and to avoid any dogged ambition.

Special books on mental techniques and suggestive learning are already available, so I will only describe those air trances that have an immediate connection to experiencing the element.

Attune Yourself to Air

Get in the right mood for an air trance by letting your mind wander aimlessly, without interpretations, and allowing your thoughts to come and go like clouds in the sky. Let your thoughts rise up, rain down, fog over, mist, and come together like cloud formations and then disperse again. Enjoy a clear view and an overview, and the ability to change perspectives at will. Let your thoughts drift, and pay attention to everything that comes to mind.

✧ What images arise when you think about these various forms of air?

◆ A breath of air

◆ A gentle wind, a breeze

◆ A draft

◆ Stale air

◆ Fresh air coming through an open window

◆ Cool night air

◆ Freezing winter air

◆ A gale

✧ What forms of thinking do these images inspire?

◆ Is it an analytical way of thinking involving separation and distinction?

◆ Is it a way of thinking that searches for new combinations and tries to overcome separations?

◆ Is it a way of thinking that proceeds continuously and leads through different atmospheres, moods, and vibrations, through different seasons and climatic zones?

◆ Is it a way of thinking that moves quickly and rapidly, and gives you surprising ideas for no apparent reasons?

◆ Is it a way of thinking that is based on details?

◆ Or is it a way of thinking that looks at everything as a whole?

◆ Is it a paradoxical way of thinking that can deal with confusion and chaos?

✧ Which thoughts have to do with the future, and what do they mean?

✧ Can you distinguish your thoughts from your wishes, feelings, and emotions? And when in everyday life are you especially dependent on your thinking?

✧ How do you move in the element of air?

✧ What would you like to take from the element of air and put into effect in your life?

Make some notes. The answers to these questions can be used for further work with air trances.

_____

_____

_____

Position of the Body: Sitting

Contrary to sitting in a crouching position, in which the chest is pressed inward and the lungs have no room to expand, here the position you assume involves stretching yourself and allowing your lungs to fill deeply with fresh air. During long sitting phases, it's a good idea to have a break every now and then, leaning back and stretching your back over the back of the chair. You can do this by resting your shoulder blades over the back of the chair and letting your shoulders hang down like a heavy coat hanger, so that the lungs can expand and spread out like wings. You can put your arms back over your head, open them, and let them hang down. The result is a position of dedication, trust, and expansion. It may remind you of flying, in which you can take pleasure in the freedom from all shackles and constraints. You can also lean your head back; this way, the front of the body—the heart, stomach, and abdomen—can expand, and the back of the body is stretched. Finally, the feet can slide forward, the legs stretching away from the pelvis as if they also wanted to glide. Now you will feel stretched out completely.

At this point, if you imagine taking a short high-altitude flight, you will feel light and carefree and be able to leave everything worrying you behind. On your return from this short but completely refreshing excursion, you will be able to tackle the tasks of daily living with new inspiration.

Visualizations

✧ Creating distance, stepping back

✧ Climbing a mountain, gaining height

✧ Looking at life as a whole—for example, as a stream flowing from its source to an estuary

Affirmations

✧ Air separates me, air connects me, and air provides the space I need.

✧ Air nourishes me, and love gives me wings. I breathe in air and love.

✧ I take the freedom I need, and give my expression to the world in return.

Trance Journeys

✧ Changing perspectives (bird's-eye view)

✧ Gaining an overview (panoramic view)

✧ A journey to the upper world (contact with your inner leader, getting advice from your inner advisor)

Trance: Opening the Inner Space

Take some time every now and then for this trance, especially if you feel overwhelmed by tasks of everyday life and have no space left for yourself, if you feel that something is choking you or you can't breathe freely anymore, if you can't feel yourself in a relationship with another person anymore, or if you feel left out.

Imagine or remember the voice that comes from inside of you when you allow space for it, the strong vibrations and sound waves of its song that are carried through space far into the world. The body knows how to affect the world around it through melody and the sound of the voice. This is true for all of us, not only opera singers. Let yourself be completely taken up by the physical feeling that comes with your voice increasing in volume and streaming forth from your mouth, continuing in a song that you recognize in the process as your very own song. It is a song that gives you power and strength, trust and pride. And while you are singing it loudly into the world, creating quite a fanfare, or softly, like an incantation, you know that you will receive a response to it, in whatever form that will reach you. While you are opening your mouth and letting your voice ring out, you know that your expression is important and makes a difference. Even if you are alone at the moment, you feel connected with all living things, which find their expression in every moment. You seem to hear the great symphony of life.

When you have this feeling of a great, all-embracing resonance, anchor it within yourself by closing your eyes, thus turning inside, and placing one hand on your stomach and feeling your own soundboard in your pelvis, while the other hand rests lightly on your larynx so that you are in contact with the strings of your instrument, with your vocal cords. Then move this hand gently down the front of your body until both hands are resting on your stomach. Conclude the trance very consciously by breathing deeply and feeling inside yourself; then slowly open your eyes.

Everyday Rituals: Making a Sound

If you have always wanted to own a valuable gong, a precious sound-bowl, or a sacred instrument like a bell, now is the time to fulfill this wish. It can be your daily ritual to make a sound with it and to listen to this sound intensively. Such a sound can signal the beginning of a phase of relaxation or a period of meditation, and with a second sound you can conclude it. Of course, you can also sing, hum, or make a sound yourself, or use any instrument you like. For the beginner, however, the ones mentioned above have proven to be the best.

Make it a rule to produce a sound every day. Concentrate on the moment when you beat the gong or the sound-bowl or ring the bell. You will be surprised at how much this sound can tell you about your present state. Are you wide open inside today and able to release the sound into the world in a relaxed way, or is the sound choked, obstinate, half-hearted, or out of key? Attune yourself to the state in which you find it best to send a sound out into the world.

When concluding this ritual, it is important to love yourself for all your sounds, regardless of how off-key, hesitant, or jarring they might be. Tomorrow is another day with a new opportunity to make another sound, and one day it will be exactly right.

Music for Air Trances

✧ Music of the spheres without rhythmic structure

✧ Bright-sounding and high-pitched sounds that can also be shrill at times

✧ Sounds from harps and sound-bowls

✧ Singing in harmony

✧ Natural sounds, like the murmuring of the wind

✧ Carefully chosen synthesizer music that artificially re-creates the murmur of the wind and gives one the feeling of the expanse of the sky

✧ Dadaist music that uses and distorts spoken texts so that new compositions are created

✧ Recitation of prayers

Further Tips

The room where air trances are practiced should be light and large, perhaps with shining parquet floors, which reflect and strengthen the light that comes into the room. The most suitable rooms are well-kept-up community halls, pleasant classrooms, and conference rooms. Chairs should be kept ready on the sidelines. You should bring a tape recorder to record the voice improvisations, because listening to your own voice will put you back into the mood you had during the trance and strengthen the effects of the trance exercise.

Space and Time Trances

In Tibetan teaching, the four elements are surmounted by a fifth one: space. It is symbolized by the crescent moon balanced on a rectangle, circle, triangle, and point, and presents itself as a vessel to the sky.

In Western countries, as well, a fifth element was added to the four known and "concrete" ones: In alchemist traditions, it was described as "quintessence"; Isaac Newton, the English mathematician and physicist, who had an affinity with the alchemists, referred to it as "ether." The main function of this fifth element is not just to contain the other four, but also to combine them in an indissoluble way with one another.

There is no reality where the elements exist separately and apart from one another—they exist together. This fifth element, which permeates all of nature, provides the connection and the continuity and is often called "space," although trances that deal with it feel quite different from air trances, where, of course, space is also discovered. Somehow it is a different kind of space that now opens up—a space beyond all space, or the center of all places. It is a spatial experience that leads us deeply into or out of (or both) the preconditions of our perception and understanding of reality. This space opens up to us when we go beyond the elements to where perception and experience begin: the consciousness.

Thus, the fifth element could be called "consciousness," or "the dimension of consciousness that becomes aware of itself," or "the space of consciousness." A person who starts a trance here never takes reality as what it seems to be. He or she always presumes that reality is a construct of our consciousness, that it has been constructed to serve as a suitable starting and landing point. Therefore, reality is not accepted as the truth, but just perceived as a point of departure.

The elements are the basis for our being anchored in reality as we know it, and as we deal with it every day. We need air to breathe, fire for warmth and light, water to drink, and the earth to stand on. We relate constantly to the elements, even though they don't exist in our consciousness in their pure form, but rather have abstract meaning and serve as points of orientation in the stream of our perceptions.

But there is a particular state of consciousness that enables us to enter the "ocean of unrelatedness," be it only for a few moments. There, the elements are dissolved; it's as if they were only crutches for our perception, and once we go beyond them, they are pushed aside. This condition is called "pure naked presence." Graf Dürckheim spoke about the "feeling of being." The being that is referred to here is, although elemental, no longer connected to any of the elements. A universal principle takes the place of distinction: that of energy.

Energy, translated literally from the ancient Greek as "effective force," builds up through all being, all forms, all contents, and all effects as continuity. We can perceive this continuum as if it was an element. We are in the middle of it—beyond the elements while still in the midst of everything that we have described as individual phenomena. It is in this state that we can experience time and space beyond the limits of normal perception.

Journeys in Trance Beyond the Usual Perception of Time

The usual time journeys that are aimed at in trance relate mostly to regressions and progressions. This means that the consciousness moves in trance to an earlier or a later point in the course of time. You could show this graphically by indicating on a straight line, representing the time line, a point before or after the present point, and then you could go there in your mind in a direct, conscious way. This method is actually quite useful. Age regressions can be undertaken in trance when the aim is to pinpoint certain traumatic experiences in a person's past and to relive them so that, after they have been made conscious again, they can be eliminated as a disturbing factor in his or her life. Abilities acquired in the past and natural talents can also be called up into consciousness by age regression, so that they are again at your disposal in the present.

In the final analysis, all learning goes back to past experiences, which we can imagine for simplicity's sake as pearls on a string. Age progressions can be pictured in the same way, but going forward in time. It's as if life is a movie that, when properly wound on a tape, could be unwound for us to see. This is an idea that is also found in the old myths, in which the goddesses of fate were represented as seamstresses busy spinning the threads of destiny.

However, time trances can also lose all direction and leave the linear dimension altogether. Then time becomes like a lake, or a sea of unrelatedness, such as that which the Tibetan Ngakpa Ch÷gyam refers to. In the midst of traveling to some point in time, you have the knowledge that you have already arrived there!

Journeys in Trance Beyond the Usual Perception of Space

Traveling beyond distance leads to the center of experience.

The dimensions of space, also, can suddenly dissolve during a trance experience. Then you find that all the precise descriptions of where you were supposed to go were in vain, as you, suddenly, without warning, find yourself everywhere and nowhere at the same time; you find that you have fallen into a paradox of space, without ever reaching the bottom of the abyss.

"Dimension" as a concept always involves the ego that measures the space. As soon as the measuring, ego has dissolved, space no longer exists. This trance is a little like the dream of the eternal fall that only ends when you wake up.

Trance journeys that are connected to a loss of the ego are, by their very nature, mystical experiences. Such journeys are not intended in psychotherapy, but they still have to be taken into consideration when they come about. In such cases, trance is no longer a means to an end, but stands as an experience in itself.

Therapists who use trance as a vehicle should be able to handle what arises if the trance goes further than originally intended. They should never forget the original objective of the trance, but they should not close their eyes when mystical experiences occur and they should be aware if it becomes useless to follow a definite purpose. The same holds true when you decide to act as your own therapist.

The breadth of consciousness enables a narrowing down of spaciousness. And only if you can accept the ego in the foreground of your being, within this sea of unrelatedness, can you calmly concentrate on a definite goal.

I know that the breadth of consciousness will not escape me, just as I will not escape from it!

PART III

FUNCTIONS OF TRANCE IN RELIGIONS

Trance and Spirituality

Most treatises on spirituality are pervaded with ideas pertaining to the separation of mind and matter that go back thousands of years; mind ranks above matter, so spirituality is regarded as better than materialism (even dialectic materialism). Back in the late sixties after the student revolts, intellectuals still tried to see the good in pragmatic and socially committed materialism, but now, especially since the fall of the Berlin Wall and the Iron Curtain, the mind has regained its former primacy.

To mention trance and spirituality in the same context seems preposterous for many advocates of mind over materialism. Nevertheless, numerous people have seen spirits during trance, which suggests that one must have something to do with the other.

The prevailing opinion relegates trance to the lower levels of primitive machinations, superstition, and magic, or regards it mainly as an instrument for manipulation. Prejudices against trance often have a historical background, as states of trance can indeed be linked to magic and superstition, and it is true that trance is also frequently used for advertising purposes and even brainwashing. Trance conjures up all too often associations with dark things that happen below the threshold of consciousness, beyond the reach of illumination. However, in the pages that follow, we will see that this limited portrayal is not always and everywhere applicable and that here, too, the boundaries are fluid.

What is trance for one person is blindness for another. And the question of who is right is often dictated by what philosophy is popular at the time or by fleeting private insights into life. The prevailing excesses of a period are best regarded as passing trends and should be viewed with a certain amount of humor. We should not lose sight of the fact that life as we know it is never static but rather subject to a constant movement up and down, back and forth. We feel our way forward, trying to see things from a higher perspective, and attempting to understand and acquiesce, although life is also a matter of preferences with plenty of opportunity for human error.

In the seventies, Carlos Castaneda's books aroused a worldwide interest in unusual states of consciousness. Suddenly, the goal was no longer meditation and achieving a tranquillity associated with the Far East, but archaic contact with the other side of reality, with the world of the spirits. Thus, shamanism appeared on the bookshelves and was offered in courses. However, it was not just a superficial, fleeting whim, but a real movement that even attracted scientists, ethnologists, and anthropologists, drawn to the strange and the mysterious. In this way, a modern understanding of what shamanism was soon developed.

Of course, it isn't entirely fair to say that Castaneda was the first to bring shamanism to the attention of the public. The cultural anthropologist Felicitas Goodman and the ethnologist Michael Harner had already published the results of their own fieldwork; still, it was Castaneda who actually started the trend.

At the same time, segments of the women's liberation movement were recalling their matriarchal heritage. These women called themselves witches again, and they gained access to trances that represented means to religious experience in archaic cultures.

Contemporary critics during this period felt prompted to display a new pleasure in the irrational. This trend, which was easily compatible with the "back to nature" orientation of those weary of civilization, could even be credited with a touch of romance. Just like romanticism, it was a response to an era of rationalism, and it represented, for many Europeans, an attempt to overcome the loss of roots of the postwar years.

In the works of the existentialist philosopher and writer Albert Camus, we find some indications of states of trance, but there trance always has the aspect of confusion, which leads to the absurd and justifies immoral acts that go as far as manslaughter.

The liberating state of ecstasy has a long tradition in French literature; it's interesting to note that some of Antonin Artaud's wildest and most beautiful texts were written in Mexico, where he became acquainted with ancient Indian customs.

The fascination with the archaic had already taken hold of the Dadaists, who frequently tried to break the bounds of reason by means of unconventional thinking, spontaneous actions, and pseudo-archaic rituals.

All these different influences and cultural levels make it difficult to clearly define terms like "trance," "ecstasy," "archaic," and "religious." In addition, these words have been misused so frequently in a new context that, in many instances, they have just become empty modern words. In recent times, attempts have been made to clear the jungle of words with the help of scientific definitions, but often the actual use of language doesn't put such new knowledge into practice. In any event, I have taken the liberty of restricting myself to the normal and accepted use of language of my own culture and of my generation (which is growing older now and has realized with surprise that young people have a completely different view of trance as well as a different attitude toward it). By the same token, I have categorized things in a way that will certainly provoke some criticism.

> In this context, I wish to differentiate types of trance by proposing three categories:
>
> ❖ the ecological, shamanic trance;
>
> ❖ the ecstatic trance, of mysticism and charismatic religious movements; and
>
> ❖ trance as a means of transformation.

In response to the frequently asked question about the difference between trance, ecstasy, and meditation, I choose to follow criteria based on the associations that these terms elicit. Trance is generally viewed as something sinister but also earthy, which brings up associations with the wilderness, with running wild, and sometimes with self-neglect. Ecstasy is connected to sex, and if this is missing, as with Saint Theresa of Avila (immortalized in a sculpture by Bernini at a moment of highest ecstatic rapture), then a suspicion of unhealthy sublimation and compensation is often voiced. Both trance and ecstasy are associated with intoxication, which is considered to be unrefined in so-called better circles. Meditation, in contrast, is thought to be exotic but still refined. After all, meditation makes no noise and is clean, it doesn't cause any kind of sensation, and it is equivalent to a voluntary self-tranquilizing. Yet anyone who has ever taken a good look at the vastly differentiating meditation practices of Hinduism,

Taoism, and Buddhism knows that such a rough summation (even if this state of tranquility is said to be proven by examining the brain waves of people meditating) is far too simplistic. Also, the boundaries between meditation, on the one hand, and trance and ecstasy, on the other, are not necessarily so clear, because these traditions have a long history that often includes an archaic or a shamanic heritage. And in the same way as certain tendencies toward wishful thinking and superstition will always exist in Christianity—and they have to exist, because they seem to be among our basic needs—so even the most civilized experiences offered by Far Eastern contemplation confront us with a confusing assortment of states of mind, which oscillate between confusion, habit, and awakening, just as life itself does.

Ecological, Shamanic Trances

The reason I have used the word "ecological" in describing this kind of trance technique is that it fits in very well with modern ecological ideals. Instead of being induced to bring about some form of good or transformation, these trances are meant to examine, heal, and maintain the global balance. Of course, they can be used on the personal level as well as on the level of a family, team, group, tribe, or modern company. However, in none of the cases where they are used does the scale pertain to anything absolute, such as an ideal, law, or virtue, to start with, but it develops. It develops from measuring. And measuring happens in trance. Only in a state of mind that is different from the usual one can the situation be perceived in a new way. This scale is used to measure the whole, which, as we all know, is more than the sum of its parts. The whole can relate to the personality with all its dark sides, the family with its black sheep, the company with its saboteurs, or the government, the nation, or the church with their heretics and dissidents.

"How do things stand with the whole?" asks the shaman, who, in the nocturnal flights of his soul, travels to those worlds that only open up in trance. These are the Under World, the Middle World, and the Upper World. Every world has its inhabitants, who meet the shaman on his mission of restoring order to a balance that has been upset. A careful approach to foreign worlds, respect, and a motivation resulting from the task set—these are the prerequisites for the success of such a mission. It's also important for the group to support the individual undertaking this journey.

The shamans were ordered by their tribes to carry out certain missions. The fate of the shaman determined indirectly that of the group.

The shamans were feared, as well as honored, and they were given food and drink, but only as long as they were successful. Therapists who see themselves as shamans have to be aware of these distinctions. They are acting on a commission. They consciously use their skill to go into trance and to travel to faraway worlds of consciousness. What they demand for this is recognition by the collective and appropriate support for their livelihood. But today, who wants to pay for something that relates to the whole as opposed to one's own personal advantage? This is a dilemma facing the modern shaman.

With more and more people demonstrating global thinking (for example, the slogan "think globally—act locally") and having a holistic view of life (such as seeing the whole as more than the sum of its parts), the concept of the whole has moved onto center stage in general awareness. What is called for are holistic interrelations, which include everything, even the universe itself. Certainly, the reappearance of ethnic shamans with their shaggy demeanor has something to do with this change in thinking, and the emergence of the new shamans is connected to the increasing awareness that the world is an ecological state of emergency. The frightening facts that present themselves on an unprecedented scale to an ecologist in satellite photos—such as the rapid changes of climate and the catastrophes in planetary balance—all help to stress the necessity of doing something. Many people feel the obligation to create balance where unbalance looms.

Our fairy tales still contain, albeit hidden beneath the surface, shamanic trance experiences. The nonhuman figures we meet there as helpers and guardians of treasures can also lead us to the "other reality." Many fairy tales are about hunters who were suddenly confronted with such figures on their expeditions and so stumbled into this other reality more or less unintentionally. There are stories in which characters fall into another reality through an ant hole or jump into it through a well shaft, as Goldmarie did in the German fairy tale of Frau Holle, or they are kidnapped by water nymphs or spirited away to the bottom of a lake. Characteristically, the latter type of tale exists in two versions: The one we know in the West ends with the tragic death of the victim, as in the German legend of the Lorelei. In other fairy tales, however, especially those from non-Western cultures, this is the beginning of a journey that concludes with a return and has a happy ending. Frequently children are kidnapped and taken to the other reality, where they are given lessons so that they can pass this knowledge on to the human collective.

The nonhuman creatures of this other reality—who, contrary to our anthropocentric views, are not only alive but also intelligent—usually have an ulterior motive in mind when they make such infringements on our world. And their motivation is usually ecological in nature. Often they want to draw attention to themselves and to their existence, which is invisible to us; they want to register certain claims, or mark certain areas as theirs, which are incompatible with our own claims, or to warn us if something is not right. The souls of slain animals appear to the bloodthirsty hunter, dwarves show the farmers where natural resources are, mermaids or seals appear to the fisherman, and Frau Holle to Goldmarie. In all of these stories, there is something we can learn. In a well-known story by the Brothers Grimm, Pechmarie (literally, "Bad-Luck Mary") is selfish and hasn't learned anything, so she is in a bad way. But this shouldn't be regarded as a punishment, but rather as a consequence of her own stupidity.

Originally, the shaman was a special person who was predestined to undertake the dangerous and difficult task of trance journeys by virtue of his natural gifts or inheritance. Today, without a doubt, there are still people who can enter trance more easily than most, but unfortunately this is no longer regarded as a talent or a mission, but all too often as some kind of impediment.

Everyone can learn to make trance journeys. Focusing our attention on rhythms can be a suitable way of getting into light trances, because it is earth-bound and not dangerous. Drumming or rattling—the beating of monotonous rhythms as well as listening to them—monotone, antiphonal singing, or the repetition of simple forms of movement, like moving from one foot to the other or rocking back and forth, all have a calming effect that leads you gently into a new world of flowing reality. However, as we are dealing here with an area that is not recognized by most people, nor by society at large, it is advisable not to try to find your way alone, but to locate a suitable teacher.

Ethnologists and anthropologists who have studied cultures where the shamanic consciousness is still intact have discovered from their field research how shamanic journeys work, what you have to pay special attention to, and what you should never do. The instructions they have laid out for us don't have to be binding, but can serve as guidelines that can help us until we find our own orientation. We can use them as hypotheses, however fabulous they may seem, and check our own experiences against them or even replace them with what we have learned from our own encounters.

Ecstatic Trances in Mysticism and Charismatic Religious Movements

Whereas shamanic trance journeys have some definite benefit and take us to the fabulous world of the "completely different," ecstatic trances are much more connected to pleasure. They have no immediate benefit for the group, actual learning remains in the background, and the figures, if you meet any at all, have no firm outline. Often they are visions of light that are so overwhelmingly bright that the human eye can only be dazzled by them. Such trances often hit a person like lightning or have the impact of a brilliant fireworks display; we only have to think of Moses' burning bush or the flaming writing of Nebuchadrezzar. It is surprising how many ecstatic trances are described in the Bible. In Christian, Jewish, and Islamic mysticism, we also find indications of such trance experiences. They often have the characteristics of fire, whereas shamanic trances are related more to the elements of water, earth, or air.

In religious or spiritual contexts, the power of fire is often alluded to as a means of getting into a state of ecstasy. Fire overcomes gravity, the inertia of mass, and the force of habit. Fire purifies, cleanses, consumes, and destroys. Unlike earth, fire knows no boundaries unless it dies. Be it the fire of passion or the fire of purified love, fire wants to flow unhindered. Fire is related to the will to expand, and it consumes the air and takes up space until there is nothing left to burn. Fire needs something to consume. The same applies to the ecstatic trance, which feeds on passion, on the power of the emotions. It takes hold of everything, ravages the body like a fever, heats up emotions, and frees the mind from the heavy vessel of matter.

This is why in alchemy fire is the real generator of all processes having to do with change.

White spirit separates out from the dull, bubbling concoction and tries to flee. Fire is behind every change that causes dormant powers to be unleashed, that transforms matter into ashes, energy into the fleeting combination of flashing light and heat. What is constant is dissolved, used up, and not replaced again. Fire wants to grow beyond its own boundaries, and by doing this, it destroys its own basis, because it burns the material that feeds it.

To produce such ecstatic trances outside of a religious or spiritual context, you need a strong willingness to surrender and a belief burning within you that something is going to happen that will not only influence your life but completely change it. In the charismatic movements of the Christian church, it is the "good tidings" that derive special urgency from the anticipation of the Day of Judgement. The heralding of the end of the world adds a narrowing touch; things seem to be coming to a head, and the person under trance is filled with agitation and excitement. Surprisingly, as I have noticed again and again, this doesn't seem to be possible without such "hysterics." People who are rather lethargic or tend toward a stoical indifference find it extremely hard to rise against gravity with their inner fire, to let themselves be taken to dizzying heights of the mind or to states where they are more impressionable than normal.

To get into ecstasy, you have to be prepared to accept your inner fire.

In my book *Play Ecstasy,* I describe four varieties of ecstatic trance:

1. The oceanic trance is an ecstasy that comes about through merging, through unification. The process of merging dissolves all differences and overcomes all borders, by sacrificing individuality in order to let the individual become part of a greater whole. The longing for unification and self-abandonment is the reason for many seemingly superficial addictive structures, in which people find themselves searching for something they can never find, at least not as a dissociated individual, which is why in addiction one strives to dissolve borders.

2. The convulsive trance doesn't appear very ecstatic on first glance, because it often results in cataleptic rigidity or even a chronically catatonic state. The convulsions and the distorted facial expressions and body postures are not really an indication of rapture, although this is nonetheless a kind of ecstatic state, whose extreme dynamics cause overexcitement, which produces the convulsions or the rigidity. The state of extreme movement can easily be mistaken for immobility, similar to the whirring wings of a dragonfly that make it seem as if it is standing still. But the apparent paralysis can be experienced as such by the person him- or herself, when he or she cannot find expression of movement.

3. The Dionysian trance is an ecstasy likened to throwing fits and raving. Dionysius, the Greek god of wine, was also called "the raving god." The extraordinary thrusts of energy become aimless and uncontrolled, blinding one to all usual conditions and limitations. This is a state of "going wild" caused by religious enthusiasm or the ultimate highs of sexual ideologies, as well, which can so stir a wild mob that it finds its outlet in a lynching. The process of stirring up, of inflammation, culminates in an ecstatic climax that can only find release in frenzied action. This kind of "mobilization" has also been used in psychological warfare.

4. The state of inner ecstasy is an ecstatic state of being inside yourself in utter silence, and it is the objective of many forms of meditation. However, with most people, it tends to be more of a calm after the storm. As the goal seems best reached by using various detours, one tried-and-tested method is to let a phase of ecstatic experience come after one of the other three trances, instead of trying to reach the high level of energy that the state of ecstasy demands of the body from a cold start. Therefore, we can see why knowledge of trance and ecstasy techniques has shown itself to be effective in meditation.

But how can you reach this inner fire when lethargy and depression are wearing you down and resignation is trying to put out the fire before you even begin?

In such a case, ritual fire trances are a viable solution. By getting more familiar with the element of fire, a growing talent for ecstasy will develop, even if it wasn't there at the beginning. In the same way as enthusiasm can grow, ecstasy can be learned.

This applies to sexuality as well. In treating problems having to do with sexuality in psychotherapy, fire trances and ecstasy techniques are especially helpful.

In my group's trance "laboratory," I discovered a way of making the lift-off easier. When I compared the course of an ecstatic trance to the so-called orgasmic curve, I saw why it was so difficult to find the take-off point. Similar to an orgasm, ecstasy doesn't overcome a person out of the blue, even if it seems to. Certain signs indicate a process that corresponds to an invisible but continual tension and charging. When the tension and charging increase—and this is caused by their own dynamics—a point is reached that can be called "the point of no return." Then, discharge is the only way of returning to a relaxed state. But this point of no return is preceded by another point, which I will call "the point of conscious (or unconscious) decision." I can practice trying to feel this point, and I can make a conscious decision as to whether I want to return and let everything remain as it was, or go on and accept the risk of experiencing something new.

To be ready for trance always means to be prepared to take risks, but nowhere is it so much a precondition for dynamics and for the underlying process as it is here. I'm going to give you an example that is also connected to a physical feeling: the first headfirst dive.

At a certain point, I have to jump. But before this point, I can still stop bouncing on the diving board and come to a standstill again. However, if I want to dive, I have to jump. And this involves finding the jumping-off point inside myself. I have to decide to do it, a hundred percent, and then jump. Possibly this is why, in philosophy, a jump is a metaphor for a change that doesn't take place gradually but suddenly. Once I have jumped, I will still emerge from the water as myself, but something basic in my life will have changed: I will have jumped!

Not only are there quantum leaps, but believers are also asked to take a leap of faith. And many times in everyday life, "jumping right in" has proven to be the only right thing to do when life was confusing, and hesitation or standing still would have not have been appropriate, nor a good idea. Thus, ecstatic trances serve to acquaint us with such jumps and rapid developments before they overtake us. Every diver knows that not only is it important that you jump but how and when you do it are also important. The how and when can be practiced beforehand, but the decision itself is an action that always happens anew and requires a certain amount of will and effort. To be able to make the jump, the body as well as the mind and the soul need to be warmed up and brought into top form. The whole person has to fight against the prevailing lethargy of the old order and break away from its hold.

In religious services of charismatic movements (the latest variety is the "Toronto Blessing"), we find a clever way of structuring an event. The service starts and ends with rhythmic singing, stamping, swaying, and clapping. The lead singer spurs the congregation on with antiphonal singing to repeat certain liturgically significant texts or just single words. One such word is "Hallelujah." Repeating it has the effect of putting the cognitive mind to sleep, so that it no longer wants to argue or dispute (as, for example, in the scholastic casuistry of the Middle Ages). Instead, festivities are planned, and spirits soar. The festive, ceremonial excitement increases, especially if the congregation expects the Whitsun experience of speaking in tongues to be the main part of the event, and sees in this special form of trance the presence of the living God. But also in a quite "normal"

service, which usually involves a very short sermon of a character more beseeching than enlightening, the main part is the propagation. The tidings spread like wildfire, reaching and uplifting people's hearts. The Whitsun story mentions flames that appeared above the heads of the apostles.

The message goes deep into the hearts of the believers and stays there, to be buried and sealed by a final conclusion. This message was made flesh, in the same way as God was made flesh through his Son, and the spark of the Spirit is enclosed in the flesh. It can be inflamed at any time. This is the real meaning of ecstatic religious services. Normal services, as well, should have this effect; they should rouse the spirit and lift it above the lethargy of everyday life, where it is imprisoned. The bond with God should be renewed and confirmed in order to revive a spiritual continuity, which can then meet the demands of daily living. When trance and ecstasy are missing from religious experience, there is little enthusiasm. Then religion may still be seen as something good, but it becomes boring.

Trance as a Means of Transformation

Trance is strongly connected to deep, radical, and fundamental transformation. Trance and transformation belong insolubly together, because it is only in trance that I am truly in contact with my potential, which enables transformation.

There are various arguments for this:

✧ Only in trance do I recognize the preconditions for all forms, and submerge to the depths of those levels where forms are created and my own life takes shape.

✧ Only in trance do I arrive at a point where I am in contact with my own unconscious programs, which have determined the different aspects of my personal destiny.

✧ Only in trance do I have the opportunity to make a new decision, because, like reality itself, I am in a condition of constant, flowing renewal, and by submerging myself in this stream through trance, I can set a new course at the crossroads.

✧ Only in trance am I in that stream of magma, in that potential of primeval matter, where creation is still so liquid that it can take on any form that I can imagine.

✧ Such an experience of my own omnipotence, which enables me to be what I want and what I think, is conveyed by very special trances, including those induced through taking the drug LSD.

In shamanism, we speak of a protoplastic ego. Proteus was an ancient Greek, not really a god from Olympus, but an archaic spiritual being who lived at the bottom of the sea. He had the power to change his appearance as he chose. Fairy tales from cultures where shamanism is still alive today have characters who changed into the stone that they touched, the moose that they shot, the fish that they threw back into the water, the eagle that they followed with their eyes. From a bird's-eye view, a character in one such story sees his mother, who misses her child, and to please her he becomes a child again. Witches could also change into animals: Magic spells bear witness to this. Thus, the protoplastic ego is an ego that wanders through, and identifies itself with, different forms without merging with them. As quickly as the eyes can move can one form be replaced by another.

A modern version of the protoplastic ego is created with video clips, whereby every feature of an original portrait, such as that of a well-known personality, can be changed by means of computer animation.

In connection with these fantastic possibilities, we now arrive at a very controversial area of trance application. Transformation by means of trance can take place voluntarily—or not. In the same way that a magician can change himself into a rabbit, he can change somebody else into a rabbit who doesn't want to be a rabbit at all. Of course, the magical change into animals is only a metaphor suggesting far-reaching changes in people without them having made an explicit and conscious decision to undergo those changes.

Time after time, people ask whether or not trance can be used to force better patterns of behavior onto people through suggestions even if those people have not agreed to such changes.

In other words, can a new program be implanted in our unconscious without our consciously assenting to it?

This is obviously the case in advertising, where the goal is to influence the potential customer or buyer subliminally. Here, "subliminal" means below the threshold of consciousness.

Thus, when you are part of modern life and connected to it through the media, you are almost always subject to some kind of influence and trance induction, whether you like it or not. Even the smallest village in the mountains or on a Greek island has a TV, and immediately modern life is thrust into your kitchen or the bar—it's a guest that is hardly noticed anymore.

Of course, you can switch off the TV, not read newspapers, close your eyes when you walk past a newsstand, and go through life with blinders and earplugs. You can also find refuge in a monastery or in a faraway ashram in Asia. But when you return, the spirit of modern times will be right there, with images that catch your attention and force their messages on you.

The only way you can strengthen your mental immune system is by looking very consciously into all the messages that have gotten across to you and how they catch on. Be aware of your own weak points, of where advertising programs can take hold and meet the structure of your needs. This way, you don't have to reject advertising and fight against the general stream of influence altogether, but can enjoy being courted instead.

Advertising is free and without obligation. No one can force you to buy anything. Allow yourself to repeatedly approach this threshold of the decision to buy, so as to get an exact feeling of what it is all about. Soon you will develop an infallible sense for seduction and realize exactly when something draws you without having to follow its pull.

You will also become immune to other kinds of messages. You can watch, listen, and understand the messages without being drawn in. De Gaulle was one of the very few world leaders outside of Germany who foresaw the consequences of the rise of Hitler, because he understood German, had listened to the German news, and had read Hitler's book *Mein Kampf*. Many other politicians, not to mention the public at large, let themselves be fooled by the Führer.

Today, the term "trance" is associated with the manipulating machinations practiced by dubious religious sects. But what is the connection between trance and the message that is being drummed in or conveyed subliminally?

We know from looking at charismatic movements that the greater the excitement, or the more pleasurable or painful the experience, the better will the spiritual content sink into the "flesh" (or the neuronal paths for processing stimuli). If an ecstasy was very strong, the program following it can hardly be eliminated at all, unless the experience was surpassed by an even stronger experience. Then, and just about only then, is elimination of the ensuing program possible. That's why traumatic experiences and conditions having to do with shock often result in extreme changes of personality. If they are connected to certain messages, they more or less burn themselves into the flesh. If the shock or the traumatic experience is repeated as strongly as, or even more strongly than, the previous experience that caused the change, then it is possible for people who have been silent for years to speak again, for the blind to see, the deaf to hear, the lame to walk. This could supply an explanation for miraculous healing: The impression made on a believer by a religious experience or a holy place can have a radical effect, especially if other people have already been healed in this way before.

Many horror stories featuring black magic and the work of the Devil incorporate the use of drugs. Drugs induce the trance that is needed for one to be drawn into the ecstatic whirlwind, be it of one's own accord, for the sheer pleasure of it, or utterly involuntarily. It is a fact that drugs are used in traditional brainwashing techniques. Since time immemorial, the holy ecstasy has been supported in a religious context. Our modern abstinence from drugs is more the exception than the rule.

However, trance can also be achieved without any use of drugs at all. If the sensitive point of a personality is touched, the person concerned can develop an addictive structure that not even the strongest drugs could trigger on their own. What is this hidden weakness that is so widespread that it seems to be a part of human nature itself?

Actually, the weak point is not to be found in the weakness of the flesh, in human nature, or in any such thing—but in the *rejection* of weakness. It is the longing for strength that captivates many people and leads them toward promised improvement.

I sometimes read the advertisements in esoteric magazines and recognize that they are also promises; as alchemy does, they promise transformation, and this is where their fascination for us lies. Of course, the transformation processes don't just promise any kind of change, but a gradual rise within a hierarchy. The alchemists transformed lead into gold, and so transmuted mass into a valuable, everlasting material that does not corrode or rust and possesses a magical glow. Who wouldn't want this? But before the change from lead into gold could be seen as a worthwhile transformation, first lead had to be devalued while gold needed to have its value enhanced. The longing that formed the basis of the strivings and the sacrifices of the alchemists

not only had to do with the firm belief in better things, and the possibility of achieving them in roundabout ways through hard work, but also with the devaluation of the original situation. This means that contempt for how things are was, and is still, a motivation in achieving transformation at any cost. Faust's famous pact with the Devil forms part of this alchemist mythology. The belief in progress can be seen as a modern version of the alchemists' longing for improvement.

"Man doesn't exist in order to repeat the same behavior patterns over and over. Man lives in order to learn." We hear this again and again. Many therapies that work with trance (here, trance is understood as a direct contact with one's unconscious) propose to shed light on old, useless patterns and the places where development, which can take many forms, can occur. In this context, what is paramount is the decision to want to learn and to develop further. But sometimes this decision feels like a strong pressure inflicted on me. I feel like I'm in a sausage factory, being pressed forward, from one form into the next, from the pure sausage material to the finished product, the sausage. What began as work on details, on precise changes in negative behavioral patterns, now more and more takes on the form of a collective measure for re-education.

Esotericism was originally the secret transformation teachings of an elite group of people willing to undertake the experiment of transformation. In many cases, they gave up everything they had—their houses, their families, their standing in society—to become pilgrims without the comforts of a normal middle-class existence. They were daring scholars, who renounced all security, to become healers, priests, and mediums, abandoning themselves wholly to inspiration, to be a channel for greater knowledge and divine energy. As time went on, the esoteric movement gradually gained a broader base, and today esoteric paperbacks can be bought at every bookstore. For the masses, for whom conventional religion no longer has much meaning, the message is this: Change yourself!

This message entails two further messages: The first is You can change yourself if you want to—and if you buy a certain book (and read it), if you pay in advance for a certain course (and take part in it), or if you attend a free introductory evening (and afterward join the sect, which, of course, doesn't call itself a sect, by immediately signing a contract). The second message, even more fatal in its effect, is The way you are now is not good enough.

Behavioral therapy viewed the individual as an accumulation of conditionings. At the same time, a learning theory was developed that enables us to benefit from our mistakes and not to repeat the patterns of our conditioning again and again, but to bring about changes of behavior through specific acts of intervention. Later humanistic psychology movements sprang up that were oriented around a potential, which every person has and which is waiting to be discovered and used. Today, more and more ideologies of promise have developed that lure people with radical and fundamental promises of change. Everything is going to change, and it's going to change immediately. This addresses a deep dissatisfaction with who we are.

The optimism of behavioral therapy as regards feasibility, which is an important requirement for any kind of learning, is increasingly connected to a dualistic, black-and-white view of the world, where only good and bad exist. Of course, it is preferable to be on the side of the good, the right, and the chosen than to be on the dark side, at the negative pole of the evil, the wrong, and the damned. But the learning entailed in behavioral therapy doesn't take place in neutral, unbiased territory, but is already oriented on a predetermined scale of values. This can hardly be called learning anymore. It is a clever form of conditioning. I think I am free, I want to become even freer, and at the same time I pull the shackles even tighter that are holding me captive. The invitation to always learn more from everything and the promise of salvation, of transcending yourself and achieving as yet unknown greatness, these combine to produce a fatal adhesive, employed by many new strategies of leadership and seduction.

The trance of omnipotence that invites you to see yourself as the creator of your personal conditions of existence is more than just a blown-up variant of the American Dream. The simple, negative trances, like those having to do with a fear of living, a childish impotence, and a feeling of helplessness and weakness, lead to rejection of the self and self-contempt. And these trances can easily become the basis of machinations that aspire to transformation at any cost, in order to flee from a state that has been devalued and is therefore humiliating, that is empty and therefore dark.

Trance and Knowledge of the Self

Psychology, the science of mind and behavior, deals with emotional relations and movements, and has always tried to find access to an unconscious that stores information about the psyche. But it can be said that a large part of what we call "psyche" is unconscious, so it can be suggested that the psyche is equivalent to the unconscious. We have certain ideas about what exactly constitutes the human soul, what it is for, and how it reacts and in turn affects the wakeful consciousness. But submerging into the depths of one's own soul can only take place in a state of trance, because the normal, causal-linear, logical wakeful consciousness is not attuned to these depths and breadths. That's why psychology has always used trance techniques to gain more knowledge about what is hidden in the soul. Of course, this is also true for self-treatment by means of self-analysis, which can likewise lead to increased knowledge of the self. The techniques of auto-suggestion are applied in order to activate self-healing powers, self-esteem, and positively charged consciousness of the self.

Since Sigmund Freud's pioneering research into the personal unconscious and the dynamics of our urges and C.G. Jung's investigation of the collective unconscious, where he discovered the unredeemed dark sides in the development of human consciousness, we now distinguish between two major trends in the psychotherapeutic application of trance. Although they come from two opposite poles, they are not mutually exclusive.

In physically oriented psychotherapy, the body is the vehicle for uncovering an undreamed-of mass of information, only a small part of which is conscious, because this information is not necessary for everyday functioning. But if I want to know more about myself, be it out of curiosity or out of need, then my body can give me access to my unconscious. It is surprising how much information is released by touch or movement (kinesthetic trances). Certain postures can bring up old behavior patterns or conditionings, and parts of the body can "remember" former injuries or traumatic experiences, and they can supply the consciousness with the appropriate information. The theory of "physical memory" refutes the generally held belief that our memories are only in the brain, tidily put away on shelves like in a library.

Only a couple of decades ago, interest centered on a theory having to do with "character armor," which formed the basis for the psychotherapy practiced according to the ideas of Wilhelm Reich. This theory maintained that certain tensions that could be detected in a person's physical appearance were attributed to a blockage in the flow of life energy, which was caused by traumatic experiences. Here, the muscles were the main protagonists. In other theories (which I have described in detail in my book *Ganzheit des Lebens [Holistic Life]*), it is the organs or certain body liquids, like that of the spinal cord, that give us information about past experiences and suffering. Such formative experiences can be recalled again through trance. By means of a physical therapy that includes the psyche, it may be possible to heal many disorders. Possibly the effects of spiritual healing, the "laying-on of hands" and healing through prayer, can be explained by this new understanding of the body as a system that stores and processes information.

Today, there is increasing talk about the memory of the cells and the tissues, as if the body had an unconscious that reached into its cells, and could be tapped and made conscious. Trance is applied to uncover the information held on this level. What do the cells think, what do the tissues remember, what do the bones know, what information is relayed by the blood? However, a complicated trance induction is not always necessary. Such questions can be addressed in an inner search process within only a light state of trance.

The work with the physical consciousness can be applied in another way, whereby the present consciousness can ask about past physical experiences. "What did you experience as a fetus in your mother's womb, when at the beginning of the birth process the waters broke and everything became alarmingly narrow around you, and there was no evident way out, because the cervix hadn't opened yet?" This question is about the experience of a prenatal phase that—similar to a primal pattern of behavior—became the model for other patterns. Stanislav Grof called such a model a prenatal matrix. Before LSD became illegal, Grof lead his patients into their bodies' memories of birth processes with the help of this drug, and discovered after years of research four archetypal formative patterns, which he identified as prenatal matrices.

"What did your mother's ovum think shortly before conception, when your father's sperm managed to get in before all the other millions of sperms?" This is roughly the kind of question asked in the whole-self psychology developed by Jon Turner. And it makes a difference what the cells thought, even before the actual conception. We are realizing more and more from research that matter has no fixed form—but is a dance of energy, a symphony of vibrations, and patterns of movement—and that matter can easily be influenced, even "dead" matter, but living organic matter all the more so. Matter is subject to the laws of the mind that forms it; it is plastic and malleable, and influenced by primal patterns.

During the search for formative primal patterns, we may even leave our present life and undertake a journey into our past lives, if this helps us (or the client) to be able to deal better with the present. Reincarnation therapy deals with phenomena (especially unfounded or excessive angst, feelings of guilt, and the like) that have no explanation in this life and may point back to formative experiences during another lifetime. The trance experience of going back in time and reliving the past situation that caused the problem or propensity is often sufficient to explain the phenomenon.

A further aspect that is pertinent here has to do with the principle of karma, according to which past actions influence our present life as long as the karma hasn't been removed. In this case, it is not enough to recognize a misdeed and to bask in the light of self-knowledge: You need to atone for it—a principle, by the way, that you also find in Christian thinking (as original sin, which is only expiated by the sacrifice of God's Son) as well as that of Judaism (with the atonement of sins on Yom Kipper). Not only can you use trance when the conscious search within is unable to uncover the origins of certain perplexing feelings, such as guilt, but also to discover the source of the karmic conditions that keep on coming into play in your life. The legends of the saints often tell of dreams that communicate a certain mission. In the same way, you can discover through trance journeys to past lives what you are supposed to do in this life. But such journeys are not necessarily advisable to undertake alone; for this trance work, it's best to seek a reliable helper and companion.

The subject of a last reflection in the search for more knowledge about ourselves has to do with the decision that led to our birth. Assuming that every life and many life sequences are preceded by a corresponding decision, then it may be interesting to find out which decision was responsible and which formative primal pattern existed. That's how we get to the matrices of the primal patterns themselves.

Is it important to know which primal pattern you chose even before you started your journey through many lives? Do your future decisions change with knowledge of past lifetimes? What benefits do you gain from a self-knowledge that goes beyond your present self?

Such questions have a bearing on what it means to be a human being, on the meaning of human existence, of human determinism, of the *conditio humana*. In this context, states of trance can certainly help us reach a higher and more rarified form of understanding. Trance can help us approach, and put us into contact with, a knowledge that exceeds the level of direct experience, and that lies somewhere above or below all possible known levels. But however close the final solution to the puzzle may seem, the approach remains endless.

Trance, Transcendence, and Awakening

According to a legend, shortly after his enlightenment, Buddha met a man in the street who was blinded by his aura. He stopped, fascinated and shaken, and asked Buddha, "Friend, what are you? Are you a heavenly being or a god?" "No," Buddha replied. "Are you then a magician or a wizard?" Again, Buddha answered no. "Are you a person?" "No." "Well, my friend, what are you then?" Buddha answered simply, "I have awakened."

In Asia, Buddhism, with its various meditation practices of awakening, took the place of older traditions, whose roots were in shamanism. These traditions not only showed an involvement with magic and superstition, but also displayed a competent treatment of natural and supernatural powers, as did the pre-Christian cultures of the West. From both, many customs have been preserved as popular beliefs. These include a value placed on a closeness with nature as well as a respect for the powers and the spirits of a place and for the energies effective in nature—ideas that were lost by subsequent "enlightened" philosophies.

It is important to know exactly what the awakening of Buddha means. Awakening is the opposite of sleeping and dreaming, and is used as a metaphor to show that a radical transformation of consciousness has taken place. In contrast to sleeping and dreaming, awakening is described as the higher, heightened, or true consciousness. This means that a development has taken place that led from one state to another. Here, too, an improvement on the scale of hierarchical values could be recorded, if such a scale existed. But it doesn't exist. There is no classification of more conscious or less conscious, but only a leap into what is described as transcendence in the West and enlightenment in the East.

Transcendence and enlightenment are by no means the same thing. But there is still a similarity, namely in regard to the relationship of everything that preceded the leap.

Transcendence is a crossing over, a process that is irreversible, because once it has taken place, it has indelibly engraved itself in our consciousness. This is a learning experience beyond all learning contexts and has to do with perception. A certain interest that wants to be satisfied is always a precondition for perception as well as for learning. The truth that is accepted and learned is always predetermined by expectations and motives. Once I have looked behind the screen on which all the usual learning programs are listed, then learning itself, as well as all the goals that I can attain through learning, will seem insubstantial to me. This experience of looking behind the screen will reduce the one-sided tension, which has established itself in my life like an overstrained spring, always directing me toward what I haven't yet learned. At the same time, a feeling of relaxation will spread inside me, making me feel soft and spacious. This is the beginning of what we understand as meditation.

Trance and Spiritual Development

As soon as the original balance has been disturbed and the world has fallen into two divisions—into good and bad, useful and useless, self and others—then trance loses its innocence and sets itself goals, becoming useful itself. Trance becomes a means and an end, and the end is magic and action. Trance also helps us have useful experiences, to which the narrow wakeful consciousness might not be receptive; trance is an aid for remembering and learning, for suggestion and manipulation. In the latter case, we need to have an ethical attitude that is able to distinguish between black and white magic. But even white magic, which commits itself to the good of all, is and remains magic. Whether self-enchantment or re-enchantment of the world (which is often called for as a balance to rationalistic disenchantment), it's always a matter of magic, of tricks, of machinations that keep the consciousness shackled to functionality. Buddha's awakening, however, represents liberation and a return to an innocence that nevertheless will never be the same as it was in the archaic consciousness of close, undivided attachment to the world. Going beyond a consciousness bound by functionality, the next step is that of "unlearning," of letting be, of accepting the world and, above all, ourselves.

EPILOGUE: TRANCE—RECONCILIATION WITH THE UNCONSCIOUS

The ego, the core of our so highly valued wakeful consciousness, which sets the standards for normality—this ego, which inflates itself into a collective "we" and thinks it can determine the course of events through its will, control, and knowledge—this ego is only an island in the sea of the unconscious. No, it is not even an island. It is a small boat on high seas, but not even that, really; it is only the helmsman who tries to steer the boat. Would it be right for a helmsman to despise the sea on which he sails? Would it be proper to look down on the means that makes this journey possible, and to feel superior to it? Would it be an advantage to scorn one's immediate surroundings, to be above taking a look at the conditions in which one travels?

The ego consciousness emerges from the background, from the undifferentiated abundance of the unconscious, and makes a difference. But the ego is still frightened that the effort of emerging was in vain, that the difference will be dissolved again. The ego has to dissociate itself so as not to get lost. The ego is flooded with fear to such an extent that it becomes rigid and has to dissociate itself in a far larger sense than necessary. The ego despises its origin, like the son who went out into the world in order to become something better. However, the time has come for reconciliation.

With respect and awareness, it is much easier for us to become familiar with the conditions of our lives. The conscious use of trance and autosuggestion can help bring us to this respect and awareness, and lead us to a true "ecology of the mind."*

* *This is the title of a book published by Gregory Bateson.*

GLOSSARY

For easier understanding, some terms are explained below. They are not, as usual, in alphabetical order, as one term follows from another.

Other Reality What is meant here is the realm of the invisible, the unusual, and the extraordinary, which we find especially in fairy tales. In the Brothers Grimm story of the same name, Goldmarie falls through the well shaft and arrives in the "lower world," the realm of Frau Holle. In ethnology, the other reality is also described as beyond-everyday, or extraordinary, reality; in psychology, it means the unconscious and the id level.

Possession This is a state in which people are no longer themselves, but are so taken over by spiritual powers that they seem to be completely different people. Gods, spirits, and demons appear within a ritually circumscribed, socially accepted, and religiously defined framework, which is part of life, even if it usually remains invisible. Felicitas Goodman points out that possession is a phenomenon that only developed with the advent of agriculture and with the increasing human control over everyday life, and that it plays a role in cults and rituals. From a cultural-anthropological point of view, possession goes hand in hand with the dualistic differentiation of inside and outside, useful and useless, belonging and foreign, good and bad, in a social system of values. In many cultures, possession is considered to be a desirable condition, because the possessed person is seen to be visited by the gods. In the Old Testament, a visitation of this sort can be of a divine nature and be valued as a state of grace and favor. In Christianity, however, we find a development occurring that leads away from the mystical feeling of being filled with the Holy Spirit; by stressing human free will, Christianity now views the Devil as the only outside force exercising any hold over human beings. That's why mystical as well as charismatic sects speak not so much of possession but rather of ecstasy when the beyond-everyday conditions of rapture and emotion arise.

Ecstasy The writings of the mystic Theresa of Avila describe this trance state, where we feel weightless and light, and which seems to lead upward rather than submerging us in the darkness. Rapture seems to happen very suddenly and rather violently; Theresa spoke of *raptus*, which is equivalent to an abduction and, similar to rape, more or less ignores the will of the person concerned. Many mystics, such as Master Eckhart, speak of a night journey of the soul, in which they describe falling into a dark chasm; this seems to be the counter-movement to the rising up, or the ascension, described in ecstasy. Just as mountains and valleys belong together, highs and lows seem to alternate in ecstasy.

Trance In this specific state, we are put in contact with the unconscious. Whether or not my ego consciousness stays fully awake or is switched off depends on the kind of trance I am in. No one can really say what the unconscious is, because it is essentially an abstraction. Sigmund Freud, for example, considered the unconscious to be a den of iniquity, resulting from inner urges that have to be suppressed in a repressive society. Thus, when contact with the unconscious is established in trance, we can assume that all those sins will present themselves that have been successfully repressed previously. Freud's entire theory rests on the repression of sexuality, because his patients had an enormous wealth of sexual fantasies. For other people, the unconscious is a hidden treasure, containing valuable resources for self-healing and creativity, and a source of inspiration. It is likely that this expectation will be confirmed in trance. Likewise, if I regard the unconscious as equivalent to the spiritual and divine inside me, I will meet this aspect in trance. Therefore, many spiritual movements and sects use trance in their services.

States of Trance These can be very different. In research into clinical hypnosis, it was discovered that hypnotic induction triggered not only states of deep relaxation, but in some circumstances, also panic, uncontrolled excitement and agitation, hysteria, convulsions, and abnormal muscle tension. The highs and lows of the mystics, with their ascensions and plunges into the night, can also be explained by different states of trance. All these states seem to be both mutually dependent in an organic curve, and to alternate in a chronological order. In most cases, a phase of inspiration is followed by a phase of incubation, which is increasingly connected to agitation. Then there follow conditions of concentration, tension, and friction, which may be experienced as paralysis, but actually represent a state of increased motion. Such conditions may even become extremely explosive, threatening to tear a person apart, and may be accompanied by fits and ravings, which may culminate in complete physical exhaustion and collapse. (This is how they are described in cases of "dance rage.") In this state of trance, a person loses control of his or her movements, so that the unconscious can run free without restriction. The running free (described by the Church Fathers as "dancing out," and forbidden by them) has a cathartic effect, and is therefore purging and liberating. As a result of the extreme pressure, a loss of consciousness can ensue, with the body falling into a state similar to a coma. Like a fever does, this extreme condition of tension causes the turnaround, the crisis that brings healing. If conditions are allowed to follow their organic course, the crisis, which is often connected to a loss of memory, is followed by regenerating relaxation, giving the organism what it needs. In this final phase, the body can recuperate and build up its defenses again.

Trance Medium This is a person who receives and mediates certain messages in trance for others. A medium is a mediator. The mediation can happen between any levels. A medium can get into contact with so-called lower astral worlds and call up irksome ghosts, or mediate the messages of the dead to their families. The medium establishes contact, but is not in any way responsible for the message, nor does the medium have any influence on the kind of being that is called up and contacted. But the medium is indirectly involved in the quality of the messages. According to the esoteric principle that maintains that things of the same nature attract each other, a weakly developed medium will only move around the lower levels of "haunting" and be used by specters. But if a medium has a high spiritual level, is motivated by compassion instead of sensation-seeking and the striving for power, and, above all, controls his or her own feelings instead of being controlled by them, then higher beings will be attracted from the hereafter, offering their wisdom to those who question and search.

Possession Cults Here, the possessed become mediums, and vice versa. In some cultures, such mediums are highly regarded. In Christian societies, possession always means being taken over by diabolical or demonic powers. Thus, in such societies possession can never be healing or inspiring or in any way improve the quality of living. Movies, like *The Exorcist,* have awakened considerable interest in the phenomenon of possession, but unfortunately this interest was not directed at the possible positive effects of possession, but maintained a fatal attitude reflecting a lack of self-determination and helplessness instead.

Demons These are beings without a body, but with a mind and a consciousness. *Daimon* was originally the name that Socrates and his pupil Plato gave to the human soul. The *daimon* in a person was the precondition for self-determination, and without it, man was said to be at the mercy of the gods. The *daimon* brought responsibility of the self into life. Thus, demons are negative aspects of the original *daimon.* Demons, in psychology, are negative aspects of the soul that are repressed, separated, and excluded from the integral soul. Such fragmentary aspects can also be found in fallen angels, as in the figure of Lucifer, who was originally a bearer of light. People are susceptible to the demonic if they have to split off, exclude, or repress too much. In trance, as used in psychotherapy, there is often mention of demons. Trance can have a healing effect as catharsis (purging) and integration (becoming whole by consciously accepting our own dark sides). In cases of demonic possession, it is absolutely vital to contact a professional and not to try to go through the process by yourself.

Hypnosis What is referred to here is the method a person uses to put another person into trance. In a therapeutic context, this happens voluntarily, meaning that the patient gives his or her conscious consent. In modern hypnotherapy, it is common to formulate something like a transfer order that also sets out the goal and the purpose of the hypnosis. Thus, the orientation of the process is given an official form, which can be transferred from one therapist to another. In this context, patients officially voice their interest in change, and also expresses what they want to be changed. These "ceremonial" proceedings supply a framework for the therapy and have a calming effect, as well as enhance and structure the healing intention. (An agreement of this kind between a therapist and a patient is also increasingly used when no hypnosis is applied. It provides clarification, and this in itself has a healing and problem-solving effect.)

The question that is always asked is whether or not people can be "magically" influenced without giving their consent. Is it possible to hypnotize people against their will?

Of course, there are people who are especially suggestive and others who are especially suggestible. It was found that the latter usually have a dissociated personality structure, marked by fragmentation, separation, and repression. This can be found in cases of schizophrenia or multiple personality. Suggestibility often develops from early childhood traumas that were not dealt with—for instance, from abuse.

People with charisma have a particularly suggestive effect on others. Great leaders must have charisma to be able to move the masses. Charisma in itself is neither good nor bad; it is a power—the power of aura, which takes effect on the unconscious level and cannot be logically explained. It works physically and is dependent on body language. People with charisma radiate that they are at one with themselves, which is exactly the opposite of what happens with a dissociated personality. This unity gives them enormous energy, which they do not have to use to hold themselves together all the time. The best means you can employ against becoming a victim of outside suggestions is to strengthen your own personality. This means becoming conscious of and accepting yourself. What is also important is having direct contact with your body, the physical part of your personality, and treating it with loving care.

Self-Hypnosis This is the means of putting yourself into trance. It is a conscious and voluntary act that requires some practice. For example, mediums who go into trance by way of self-hypnosis (like Edgar Cayce) have developed their own special methods. The techniques you will use depend on the type of person you are, what you respond to most strongly, and which of your sense channels finds it easiest to get into contact with the unconscious. Self-hypnosis requires techniques of concentration and relaxation, as they are practiced in yoga, meditation, and other spiritual disciplines, including Silva Mind Control and other mental techniques for improving one's performance, as well as autogenous training. Such techniques help you to put yourself into a light trance, which can be very helpful in many everyday situations. Of course, it is also possible for you to go into a deeper trance. Such slip-ups can occur, as the unconscious is not tidily put away in drawers, but has a life of its own. You may just want to relax deeply, but in the process find yourself having a bright vision of the future. Or, you may use self-hypnosis at the dentist's office in order to deal with your fear and pain, and this can put you unexpectedly into a euphoric state, the likes of which you have never experienced before. In this state,

you may find yourself confronted with unknown areas of yourself that frighten you more than the dentist's drill. However, if you have a conscious personality structure, which you look after, and if you value and unconditionally accept yourself, you will be protected against splits of personality. Don't forget that everything that happens is all a part of the process, and all a part of you, otherwise it wouldn't have happened to you.

Autosuggestion This is different from self-hypnosis in that, although you use the same powers to get into a changed state of consciousness, you don't necessarily do so consciously. In fact, the less you consciously know, the more effective the suggestion can be. It affects the unconscious, and the unconscious doesn't want to know anything, but wants to be impressed. The best example is the placebo effect: If you know that a certain pill is a placebo, it is not likely to have the same effect on you as it would if you didn't know it. In this case, knowledge cancels out the effectiveness, as your unconscious says disappointedly, "What, only a placebo? It takes more than that to impress me! I need something stronger!" The stronger medication is always one that doesn't require a decision from the ego consciousness. It appeals directly to the unconscious. The ego should take a vacation and relax. It deserves it, after all the control it has to exercise day after day!

By the way, the ego on vacation is a vivid picture that allows and supports autosuggestion with the complete agreement of the ego, which hasn't been ignored but is just resting. The ego leaves the competence for autosuggestion to the unconscious, because it realizes that sometimes delegation is more effective than effort in certain areas of life. The placebo effect is frequently described as less than something that is real. A therapy or comparable technique is said to be effective "only" on the level of a placebo, meaning not effective in reality. But reality is created by us and develops in our own brain, and all too often without the help of conscious will and the logical mind. The powers of suggestion are extremely creative and powerful. Probably more people have been healed with the placebo effect than with so-called real intervention.

Monoideism and Monotony These terms refer to traditional techniques of trance induction. In monoideism, a single idea is thought repeatedly in the form of a sentence or a symbol. An example of monotony is one sound or note being repeated without using the other notes in the scale.

Hallucination This usually describes a symptom that can occur with certain diseases. However, a hallucination can also be reinterpreted to be an ability. It is the ability to imagine something that cannot be experienced in the present reality because it doesn't exist. It only exists in the imagination. But even this imagined existence can have a healing effect if the products of your imagination do you good. Controlled hallucination is a trance technique in Neurolinguistic Programming (NLP), through which, with the help of fantasies, you can put yourself into situations by imagining them. Controlled hallucination is not a talent or a heavenly gift; it has to be learned and practiced to achieve mastery. The means used is the power of the human imagination, which is a kind of thinking, and actually makes thinking as a complex process possible. Imagination and visualization are ways of thinking that are called for when using trance for therapeutic purposes. However, this makes particular demands on clients: They need to have a certain power of concentration to be able to bring their imagination into play. Thus, many trance techniques are only suitable for some people. They don't have to be intellectual or educated, but they have to be able to concentrate, stick to the subject being dealt with, and call it to mind at will. People who are not able to do this should look for outside help when they have problems and not push themselves too far by trying to heal themselves through autosuggestion. Asking for help simply means falling back on another powerful trance induction, the contact with another person.

Rapport and Transfer These are the types of contact between the hypnotist and the hypnotized that work best and actually make trance possible. Harmony and affinity make the relationship easy and help the hypnotized avoid putting up blocks. "Transfer" is a term used in psychoanalysis, and means the carryover of learned responses from one type of situation to another, but in the context of psychoanalysis it has nothing to do with hypnosis. Sigmund Freud also worked with hypnosis in the beginning, but then developed his own technique, which he was convinced allowed the patient more freedom. This is the method of free association, whereby the patient lies on the proverbial couch and the analyst sits beside him or her, pencil poised in hand. Freud had realized that in hypnosis his own expectations affected his patients and brought forth from their unconscious what he had more or less expected. That's why he changed his approach to the unconscious by replacing the traditional, hypnotic swinging pendulum and colorful moving light with his own technique of free association, by which scraps of thought, inner pictures, and emotions would arise, giving access to the unconscious. He may have been of the opinion that speech would prevent his patients from going into too deep of a trance, which would once again subject them to the suggestive powers of his own expectations. Here, however, Freud was off the mark, because in every successful communication suggestive powers take effect, and expectations always have a bearing on perception.

Analysts have to take care not to interfere. The analytic technique only works if the patient alone is the center of attention and can unrestrainedly project the relationship patterns of his or her early childhood onto the analyst so that they can become conscious and are assimilated; for this reason, it is important for the analyst not to get involved in this relationship trance. But more modern trends in psychotherapy regard this abstinence as impossible, for, as Bateson says, "I can't help communicating." This is even truer for a technique that depends so heavily on contact. The transfer itself is the trance. Hypnotherapists speak about a model based on a form of Socratic questioning, characterized by its especially emphatic and continual obstinacy, but also gentle enough to allow the patient to enter the search process by interrogating him- or herself. But once the patient is in the state of this penetrating and thorough self-questioning, he or she is already in trance. So, when this method is used in hypnotherapy and NLP, the transfer that takes place in psychoanalysis is replaced by personal contact.

Resonance Originally a term in the field of acoustics, resonance means the intensification and enrichment of a musical tone by added vibration. In a figurative sense, it has to do with a quality evoking response or feedback; a message that finds resonance can thus take effect, set something in motion, and cause vibrations. In the holistic view of life, in quantum medicine, and in system-oriented psychotherapy, the term "resonance" refers to a certain deep understanding or sympathy. In these contexts, resonance leads away from the two-dimensional way of thinking in linear, causal connections to new dimensions of vibratory fields and connections of entities in a network. Resonance is a form of contact that does not refer to an individual or an isolated part, but to the whole; when a single part is touched, the whole starts vibrating. The echo doesn't reflect exactly what was said, but acts as a soundboard. What returns has gone through a feedback loop and now represents something new. This kind of understanding, as described by resonance, goes beyond the usual understanding that takes place on a rational, logical basis. It is a physical resonating, which psychotherapists also refer to as "empathy." The therapist is unable to detach him- or herself if he or she truly wants to understand the patient, and has to enter the same mood as that of the patient. Likewise, the mood and the vibrations of the therapist (and also his or her expectations) affect the patient.

Hypnotherapy, as Developed by Milton Erickson
Milton Erickson (not to be confused with the developmental psychologist Erik Erikson) is the founder of hypnotherapy, although he himself never wrote any books about his work or developed any theories about it. He was an extremely successful psychotherapist who solved even the most difficult problems and conflicts, including his own, in an extraordinarily light and playful way. When he suffered from polio in his youth and was told by a doctor that he would die early, he was determined to pit his own will to live against the medical diagnosis, and he came out the victor. Obviously, he had discovered a strategy of self-healing. According to reports of patients, colleagues, and students, Erickson had a very unspectacular approach, which mostly consisted of the telling of strangely complex stories. This form of hypnosis was completely different from the clinical hypnosis that worked

with pendulums and suggestive voices. When Milton Erickson died as an old man, many schools of psychotherapy were founded that used hypnosis and trance therapy in a completely new way.

Milton Erickson's Hypnotherapy and the Systematic Approach The Milton Erickson Society offers courses in Europe and strives to uphold a theory worthy of the practice of this brilliant pragmatist. Gregory Bateson describes the approach of system theory in his book, *The Ecology of the Mind.* The basic understanding that everything is somehow connected with everything else and influences everything within a system, the interactions being of a complex and unpredictable nature, receives a new meaning if the aim is to develop a new style of therapy or to explain its effects. The Milton Model, as this new style is called, distinguishes itself by its special way of dealing with complex contents; instead of trying to diagnose, define, and explain the patient's problems, and to find their origin, it just tries to cause changes. But this doesn't occur in the usual way, as in behavioral therapy, by addressing the problems directly, but through a complex method of communication on various levels. Such multilevel communication includes jokes, stories, playful intervention, experiments, and everyday rituals. As everything is connected to everything else, a positive change will affect the whole system. The system can be the complexity of a personality, but it can also relate to a family, a team, or even to the whole social structure. The system can even include the environment, and in this respect, can actually become an ecology that starts in the mind. This would then provide a link to shamanism.

Shamanism and Psychotherapy In the past, the archaic religion of shamanism was often viewed condescendingly as a primitive forerunner of the so-called high religions. But today when complex interrelations are calling more and more for an ecology of the mind, religious forms of dealing with the world as well as the environment are being rediscovered. One such form is animism, whose spiritual leaders are shamans. In animism, the whole world has a soul; that's where the name comes from, as the Latin word *anima* means soul. Even nonhuman forms play a role in the great system of nature and life. If a change occurs somewhere, it has an influence on everything else, including humans. Human beings are no longer at the center of the universe, but they stand in the midst of everything. We do not exist independently of everything and everyone, and neither are we completely dependent. "Interdependence" is a term that does justice to the systemic approach as well as to the new understanding of shamanism. Systemically oriented psychotherapies find it easy to adopt elements of shamanism and to apply them playfully. The journey to the personal unconscious—for instance, to contact the "powerful beast" within—is even undertaken with children. But adults also react positively to these journeys of discovery, and can learn things they previously wouldn't have thought possible. The understanding of reality grows constantly in the process. In the future, trance will no longer be a curiosity reserved for weirdoes, but will develop into a generally recognized vehicle for those who are eager to learn and have an open mind.

Freaks and Freak Shows These were the great sensations in Victorian times. Public interest was aroused by everything that didn't comply with the norm, starting with physical disfigurements. The famous Elephant Man as well as giants and dwarfs and others exhibiting abnormalities were a constant a source of fascination. During the hippie movement, those who had unusual interests or habits outside the mainstream culture (such as drug trips) were called "freaks."

Convulsions These are uncontrollable fits that have a cathartic (cleansing or liberating) effect. In the 19th century, in particular, convulsive trances were very much in vogue, and trance séances were frequently filled with melodrama and hysteria.

Liquefaction This is a metaphor that tends to be used in trance work for the dissolving of boundaries and fixations, as the unconscious is assigned to the element of water.

Neurolinguistic Programming (NLP) This has rapidly gained a foothold in the areas of psychotherapy, economy, and education. In the broadest sense, NLP means learning on the level of neuronal channeling; it is on this level that conditioning, as a way of unconscious learning, affects a person's behavior, attitudes, views, beliefs, and philosophy of life. The force behind NLP was again Milton Erickson, together with the family therapist Virginia Satir and the founder of Gestalt therapy Fritz Perls. The model was developed by two young students of information technology (Bandler and Grindler), whose aim was to gain access to more successful strategies. Information technology deals with the transfer of information that manifests itself on the level of conscious development as learning. The ecology of the mind aims principally at using experiences as a means of constant learning and relearning. In psychotherapy and education as well as in management, a successful intervention has to take a critical look at how a person or a team can learn from their experiences, in order to make the best possible use of what they have learned. In this case, mistakes are nothing more than a useful source of feedback, and a fundamentally optimistic attitude is predominant, emphasizing learning as a basic impulse of the dawning of consciousness. Especially in connection with processes of molding and conditioning, as well as constructive, goal-oriented learning, and open-minded further learning and relearning, trance is of decisive importance.

De-hypnotherapy is an interesting attempt to rename the already existing and flourishing new school of hypnotherapy in order to endow it with a spiritual perspective. Followers of the spiritual leader Rajneesh Bhagwan founded a free university in Poona, India, where new approaches to humanistic and physical psychotherapy were taught. All kinds of trance induction and techniques were the basic requirements for new professions, which were created here as a synthesis of East and West. According to the Eastern philosophy of life, hypnotherapy is based on the assumption that basically everything is illusion and that the "Real Being" only shows itself through meditation on the intrinsic level of essence. In the end, every normal orientation to a goal, all striving for material fulfillment, all ambitions for success and productivity, are only food for the demon of deception. The world is an illusion and reality a dream. We are all in trance, we float from one trance to the next, and real consciousness only occurs during fleeting moments of awakening, which can be nourished through meditation. But trance is not fought against, but is used here, too, as a means to an end. The more we are aware of our everyday entanglements, the more we understand the ways of trance and where they lead us. In the end, we are in full command of our personal spiritual life, without taking it too seriously. In the transition to spiritual experiences, we can consciously distance ourselves and enjoy life to the full without falling prey to individual sorcery and deception.

Disenchantment of the World Coined by the sociologist of religion Max Weber (1864–1920), this term denotes the devaluation and dissolving of religious traditions in an era of Enlightenment and rationalism. Weber warned of the consequences of a mechanistic and nationalized philosophy without a binding force to give it a meaning. Morris Berman takes up the subject again with a plea for a "Re-enchantment of the world," which is also the title of his book. This re-enchantment would be equivalent to a second Enlightenment.

BIBLIOGRAPHY

Ackermann, Diane: *A Natural History of the Senses,* New York 1990.

Hoffman, Kay: *Play Ecstasy,* Südergellersen 1992.

Hoffman, Kay, Haberzettl, Martin, and Schneider, Maria: *Body-Mind Management,* Paderborn 1996.

James, Tad, and Woodsmall, Wyatt: *Timeline. NLP Konzepte,* Paderborn 1992.

Lankton, Steve: *Practical Magic: A Translation of Basic Neuro-Linguistic Practice into Clinical Psychotherapy.*

Rossi, Ernest Lawrence: *The Symptom Path to Enlightenment: The New Dynamics of Self-Organization in Hypnotherapy,* California 1996.

Spiegel, Herbert, and Spiegel, David: *Trance and Treatment: Clinical Uses of Hypnosis,* New York 1978.

ACKNOWLEDGMENTS

I owe a particular debt of gratitude to my teachers:

Felicitas Goodman (archaic ecstasy techniques)
Evi Laurich (shamanic trance techniques, from Michael Harner)
Varda Hasselmann and Ninshanto Schäfer (mediums in trance)
Jon Turner (whole-self psychology)
Jacques Donnar (trance dance therapy)
Jabrane Sebnat (trance dance and Sufism)
Reinhard Flatischler (rhythm)
Tarab Tulku (energy work in Tibetan Buddhism)
Gunter Schmidt (Milton Erickson's hypnotherapy)
Rudl Kapellner (mind machines and mind management)
Bernd Isert and Martin Haberzettl (NLP)
Bettina Spencer (systemic family therapy)
Ernst Lawrence Rossi (new approaches to dynamics and self-organization in hypnotherapy)
Matthias Varga von Kibed (creative open-mind-edness)

All of them provided me with important ideas, which I have integrated into my work and passed on in turn to others.

ABOUT THE AUTHOR

Kay Hoffman was born in 1949 and grew up in the cultures of both America and Europe; first she studied music, especially composition, and then philosophy, with an emphasis on semantics. After that, she worked as a textile designer in Italy. Upon returning to Germany, she dedicated herself to her love of dancing and made it her profession by helping groups of people achieve their individual mobility. This was how she became acquainted with various forms of trance, which proved to be very useful in therapy and work involving experience of the self. Her research into trance with regard to African trance-dance cults, and her work with shamanism, spirituality, and mediums, as well as modern methods of hypnotherapy as developed by Milton Erickson, were enriched by her travels to Brazil, Cuba, West Africa, and Morocco. Since 1980, she has been working as a writer, a consultant, and a trainer at institutes for psychotherapy and management, and is well known through her participation in many conferences on the subject of trance.

In adult education, she runs on-the-job courses in the integrative, constructive application of trance techniques in modern everyday life. For more information, contact:

Kay Hoffman
Freischützstrasse 110/803
81927 München
Germany
Phone: 089/952336
Fax: 089/952446

INDEX